The Invisible Border

The Invisible Border

Latinos in America

Samuel Roll, Ph.D.

Marc Irwin, Ph.D.

INTERCULTURAL PRESS

A Nicholas Brealey Publishing Company

BOSTON • LONDON

First published by Intercultural Press, a division of Nicholas Brealey Publishing, in 2008.

Nicholas Brealey Publishing
20 Park Plaza, Suite 1115A
Boston, MA 02116, USA
Tel: + 617-523-3801
Fax: + 617-523-3708
www.interculturalpress.com

Nicholas Brealey Publishing
3-5 Spafield Street, Clerkenwell
London, EC1R 4QB, UK
Tel: +44-(0)-207-239-0360
Fax: +44-(0)-207-239-0370
www.nicholasbrealey.com

Printed in the United States of America

12 11 10 09 08   1 2 3 4 5

ISBN: 978-1-931930-63-5

Library of Congress Cataloging-in-Publication Data

Roll, Samuel, 1942–
  The invisible border : Latinos in America / Samuel Roll, Marc Irwin.
      p.   cm.
  Includes bibliographical references.
  ISBN 978-1-931930-63-5
1. Hispanic Americans—Social life and customs. 2. Hispanic Americans—Social conditions. 3. Hispanic American families. 4. Intercultural communication—United States. 5. Culture conflict—United States.
6. Hispanic Americans—Cultural assimilation. 7. United States—Ethnic relations. I. Irwin, Marc. II. Title.
  E184.S75R675 2008
  305.8968'073--dc22   2008018777

This book is dedicated to our parents, Jaime Roll and Bertha Agudelo Roll and Lee and Lauretta Irwin, who taught to us the riches of our cultures; and to our wives, Elizabeth Jaffe Roll and Colombina Rodriguez Irwin, who have shared with us the riches of theirs.

Contents

Acknowledgments

We gratefully acknowledge the many improvements to *The Invisible Border*, which resulted from careful readings by Patricia O'Hare, the editorial staff of Intercultural Press, and Gabriela Irwin. We are equally grateful to our secretaries, Starla Hales and Linda Korte, who prepared endless drafts of the book, and to Esteban Irwin, for contributing its title.

The Invisible Border

In photographs taken from space, the earth appears as a peaceful, undivided sphere of blue oceans and lands without boundaries. That view of an undivided earth is misleading, because our world is criss-crossed by national borders which divide us.

One such border divides the United States from Mexico and the rest of Latin America. Like most political boundaries, it is a permeable one; U.S. goods, business travelers, and tourists flow south from the United States, while Latin American goods and Latinos, mostly seeking employment, an education, or a better life flow north into the U.S.

The influx of Latinos into the United States has created confusion for factory foremen in California who may be unsure how to supervise workers from Central America, for teachers in Pennsylvania whose classes now include Mexican children, and for doctors and nurses in Kansas who are asked to treat Latino patients with names and customs different than those whom they are used to treating. This book was written to help those who work with Latinos to do so more effectively, as well as to help other Americans better understand Latino culture. It was also written to help Latinos who may be new to the United States, improve their understanding of mainstream American culture.

The Rio Grande is the major physical dividing line between Latin America and the United States. An invisible cultural border also divides Latinos and those in the mainstream U.S. culture. Those in the mainstream are commonly called Anglos in the U.S. Southwest, and we will use that term in this book. It is interesting to note that Latinos and Anglos differ to a surprising degree in their values and their behavior, even though both groups have origins in Europe, are largely Christian, and share a history of colonial struggle to achieve independence.

Recently estimated at nearly 43 million, the U.S. Latino population now exceeds that of African Americans (U.S. Census Bureau 2005), and is growing more than six times as fast as the U.S. population as a whole (García 2003). With a disposable income believed to be nearly a trillion dollars a year (Chong and Baez 2005), the economic impact of U.S. Latino population growth is enormous. The political impact of Latinos in the U.S. has become equally great. Candidates for office at the local, state, and national levels are wooing the growing number of Latino voters, whose votes now can potentially decide elections.

Latinos and Anglos Are Different

The differences between Latino and Anglo values and behavior have been experienced firsthand by each of the authors. Samuel Roll is a Colombian whose family moved to the United States during his childhood. While growing up, he struggled to understand the strange ways of his new country. Marc Irwin is an Anglo who moved to Guatemala as a young research psychologist. It was equally difficult for him to understand his adopted country.

Samuel Roll recalls:

Raised as a Colombian, I had been taught that I should assist my friends when they needed help. When one of my classmates at school in the United States who had not studied the night before asked me for help during a test, I gave him answers. The teacher saw me do this, and sent me home in disgrace for cheating, even though giving test answers to other students is common and is mostly tolerated in Latin American schools.

I was confused by what I took to be rudeness in the United States. When I visited my friends' homes, their parents never inquired about my family's health. Nor did they usually offer me anything to eat, even if they were eating. My family always inquired about the families of our guests, and we always offered them something to eat or drink. In fact, we offered three times, so that guests knew that we really wanted them to accept.

I was surprised by the fact that boys and girls in the United States were treated so much alike. When my parents found out that my sister and I had joined in a neighborhood game of Spin the Bottle, my sister was punished and forbidden to play with the other children involved, but I was not. The parents of the other girls who had played did not punish their daughters. When my sister and I hit each other, I was punished, but she was not. Yet, when my friend got into a fight with his sister, both were punished equally.

I was surprised by the way business was conducted in the United States. I had watched my parents spend a long time establishing personal relationships with those they did business with, and I expected more conversation than "Have a nice day" from storekeepers and salespeople.

I was confused by the way my classmates approached their schoolwork. They would raise their hands and guess if they didn't know the answers to the teacher's questions. It surprised me even more that our teachers not only encouraged us to guess but also to believe that a question could frequently have more than one right answer. I had been taught that a question had only one right answer and to be much less optimistic about figuring answers out for myself.

Marc Irwin recalls:

As a well-brought-up Anglo, I had been taught to obey every law, and I was unprepared for the relaxed approach to traffic laws I encountered in Guatemala. I amazed my Guatemalan friends when I dutifully stopped at each stop sign or red light when there were no other cars in sight.

I was also used to a more cautious approach to making friends than I encountered in Guatemala, and I was surprised by the warmth and spontaneity of people I met there. At first it made me feel suspicious of people's motives when they invited me home and treated me like a member of the family immediately after meeting me.

Accustomed to more equality and similarity between the sexes, I was unprepared for the intense femininity of Latino women and the frank enjoyment that Latino men took in their machismo. No one seemed to worry about sexual harassment there. In fact, the air felt charged with sexuality, and it seemed to me that flirting was a world-class art in Guatemala.

I was confused by people's work styles in Guatemala. The employees of the research institute where I worked seemed to spend a large part of their time socializing, and those who did not were considered antisocial. Yet, when a deadline approached, the same employees worked almost to exhaustion, without complaint, to successfully get the job done.

I had similar difficulty understanding my Latino scientific colleagues' approach to their research. They seemed less organized and efficient in their efforts, and relied more on intuition than U.S. scientists. However, the results of their efforts were often brilliantly creative.

Who Are They? What Are We?

The differences in values and behavior the authors experienced on moving between Latin America and the United States have their origins in the cultures of Latinos and Anglos. A group's culture is summarized in their language, stories, art, and music. Every culture represents a unique version of the complex processes through which human personality comes into being. We become full human beings through being reared as members of an ongoing society. Children learn to become carriers of their culture. They share with others in their society values, ways of seeing the world, skills and knowledge, and a sense of community.

As we have noted, in this book we follow the common practice in the Southwestern United States of referring to U.S. mainstream culture as Anglo culture. The term *Anglo* is a Latin prefix used to denote English, but we use it here to include all native-born North Americans of European descent, as well as those members of all other races who have become a part of U.S. mainstream society.

The earliest non-Spanish Europeans to settle in what was to become the United States came from England and the Netherlands.

Attracted by reports of great economic opportunity and religious freedom, they were soon followed by other Europeans. Waves of Swedish, German, and Irish immigrants came in the first half of the nineteenth century to escape famine and social turbulence triggered by the industrial revolution. During the late 1800s, emigration patterns shifted from Northern and Western Europe to Southern and Eastern Europe, and large numbers of Italians, Greeks, Russians, Hungarians, and Poles began arriving in the United States, along with Eastern European Jews (Tichenor 2007).

Few Africans emigrated to the United States voluntarily, with most African-Americans tracing their ancestry to the slave trade. Asian immigrants to the U.S. first arrived in large numbers from China during the California gold rush of 1848. Thousands more Chinese laborers were brought to the U.S. during the 1860s to work on the construction of the transcontinental railroad. Restrictive legislation slowed the influx of Asians during the first half of the twentieth century, while Europeans continued to arrive in large numbers, but during the last third of the century, legislation permitting the entry of persons fleeing communist persecution resulted in Asian immigration for the first time surpassing European immigration (Federation for American Immigration Reform 2007).

The cultural values of the young nation had come primarily from England. Despite the fears of anti-immigration groups such as the "Know Nothings" that new arrivals would destroy American culture, each immigrant group eventually adopted the cultural values of the English and other early European immigrants, while adding their own cultural variations. For example, Irish and Italian Americans brought a greater love of ceremony and more emotional expressiveness than earlier arrivals when they migrated to the United States.

Latino culture is shared by a varied collection of people living both in the United States and in Latin America. The term Latino is frequently used in the U.S. interchangeably with Hispanic, though there is controversy over which term should be used. We have chosen to use the term Latino because it is a Spanish language word and clearly refers to residents of Latin America (Garcia and Sanchez 2007), though we respect the preference of some for the use of the term Hispanic. Core cultural values of this group originated in Spain and were brought to the New World by the Conquistadors.

Most of the Spanish Conquistadors took Indian wives, creating the Mestizo population, which numbers more than half of all Latin Americans. The remainder are primarily of European or pure Indian descent, and Black and mixed-race individuals who are the descendents of African slaves brought to Latin America, plus a small number of Asians. Europeans are concentrated in Argentina, Chile, Costa Rica, and Uruguay. In some Latin American countries, such as Costa Rica, there are no surviving Indians. They were either taken as wives or killed off by the Spanish at the time of conquest. The Black population is mostly concentrated in the Caribbean.

Latin American countries are also economically diverse. Many depend on a few export crops, and for Bolivia and Colombia, the value of illegal drug exports, while not precisely known, may equal or exceed that of other exports (Potter and Farthing 2000, North 2002). Other countries, such as Argentina, have developed an impressive industrial base, while Venezuela and Mexico have produced great wealth from the sale of oil. Within the richest and poorest Latin American countries a dramatic gap exists between the rich and the poor.

Politically, the region has been plagued by instability, with frequent, often violent, changes of government. Current governments run the gamut from true democracies, such as Costa Rica, to many nominal democracies that fall short of true majority rule and protection of individual rights, to dictatorships of the left and the right.

Varieties of Latinos

According to recently adjusted figures based on the 2000 U.S. census, the majority of Latinos in the United States, approximately 63 percent, are of Mexican origin, and some of these individuals can trace their roots back to as far as the sixteenth century. Another 10 percent of U.S.

Latinos are Puerto Rican, and 4 percent are Cuban. The remaining 23 percent have their origins in the other 17 largely Spanish-speaking countries in Central America, South America, and the islands of the Caribbean (Garcia and Sanchez 2007).

Although this book focuses on the cultural consistencies that unite Latinos in the United States, it is important to remember that Latinos are not homogeneous, and that differences in typical behavior and values can be found across their countries of origin and also within them. For example, though appreciation of artistic expression is found throughout Latin America, no other Latin American country can match the richness and variety of visual art seen throughout Mexico.

In contrast, citizens of Chile and especially Argentina typically place a greater emphasis on the written and spoken arts. Argentina boasts an impressive number of publishing houses; her writers, such as Jorge Luis Borges and Julio Cortázar, are considered national heroes and even blue-collar workers pride themselves on being well-read.

Latinos in Cuba, the Caribbean islands, and the coast of Latin America, influenced by African culture, demonstrate less interest in the visual or verbal arts, and more in music and dance. It is almost impossible to attend a party in coastal Venezuela or Colombia or Cuba where the focus is not on music and dancing. By contrast, you are much more likely to find partygoers in Argentina or Chile engaged in lively debate or discussion.

Latin American countries also differ in the degree to which they identify with the cultures of their indigenous populations. Mexicans are fond of saying "*todos somos indios*" (we are all Indians), and Central Americans (except those in Costa Rica), Peruvians, and Bolivians also typically express pride in their indigenous heritage. By contrast, Argentineans, nearly all of whom are of European descent (Velez 1990), as well as citizens of Chile and Uruguay, emphasize their European origins.

Variability can also be found within Latin American countries. For example, in Colombia residents of the Antioquia region are proud of their reputation as entrepreneurs, and it is even common for Antioquian children to independently engage in money-making enterprises such as setting up roadside stands to sell pastries, Christmas decorations, or other merchandise to passers-by. Antioquians also pride themselves on the beauty and purity of their Spanish and prize fine sentence structure and elocution.

By contrast, coastal Colombians in cities like Cartagena and Barranquilla seem more careless about their language. Coastal Colombians clip off the ends of words, and they frankly describe themselves as blunt. In this part of Colombia there is also less interest in commerce, and many businesses are in fact run by entrepreneurs who have migrated from Antioquia.

Given the diversity among Latinos, as well as that among Anglos, who are no more homogenous than Latinos and differ by region, religion, and economic level, legitimate objections can be raised to generalizing about either culture. However, in important ways every Latino is like every other Latino, and every Anglo is like every other Anglo. Members of each group share a core culture with major points of consistency. That shared culture contains similar social organization, childrearing practices, and values. This consistency facilitates easy communication among Latinos across national boundaries and among Anglos across regional, religious, and economic ones.

Latino and Anglo cultures have important differences both in their histories as well as in their basic assumptions. The genius of Anglo culture has been in its ability to generate movement and change. People nurtured in few cultures have traveled so far, so fast as those originating in Europe, whose history contains repeated examples of migration to avoid social or religious prejudice or restriction. Those who followed the early European immigrants to the United States also demonstrated their optimism and willingness to take risks. Though few geographical frontiers now exist on this planet, Anglo culture continues to idealize unlimited freedom and opportunity.

The genius of Latino culture has been in its ability to endure. It has been sustained by a powerful attractive force that has maintained considerable continuity, and kept its flock within the fold. The attractive force of Latino culture is also seen in its ability to assimilate new members. The "melting pot" that is so often associated with the United States may, in fact, be more powerful in Latin America. Most immigrants to Latin America soon resemble native-born peers. Their children are difficult to distinguish from other Latinos.

What Happens at Home Does Not Stay at Home

The principal vehicle for transferring the values and information making up a culture is the family, a unit which exists in some form in every society. There are other important vehicles for cultural transmission as well. These include the church. For example, by having only male clergy, the dominant Catholic Church of Latin America communicates its values about how gender differences should be viewed. Other such vehicles include schools, most of which are segregated by sex in Latin America. Language also serves as a vehicle for cultural transmission, tying the culture together, and creating values and beliefs both through its structure and its body of literature.

However, it is the family, with its particular structure, that represents in its purest and most powerful form the medium of cultural transmission. To understand differences between cultures, it is first necessary to examine the differences between typical families in each culture.

One major way that families vary is in the extent to which they are hierarchically organized, with a single leader and a chain of command. Most Latino families follow this pattern, with the father clearly defined as head of the family. By contrast, the typical Anglo family is more democratic, with power shared by both parents, and children allowed to participate in decisions affecting the family.

Latino and Anglo families also differ in their degree of interdependence versus independence of family members. Independence is not usually encouraged in Latino children, whereas Anglo children are encouraged to become independent beginning in infancy, and this encouragement continues until they leave home as young adults.

A Preview of the Book

Latino-Anglo differences in family structure help to shape differences in children's adult values and behavior. The first section of this book, Latino and Anglo Families, takes a closer look at the workings of the typical Latino and Anglo families. The second, Latino-Anglo Cultural Differences, explores the differing approaches to gender, friendship, morality, religion, and thinking that Latino and Anglo families produce.

While the focus of the book is on how Latinos who are living in the United States view the world and how they behave, many of our examples of Latino values and behavior will come from Latin America. When Latinos migrate to the United States, they bring their culture with them, and to understand Latinos it is useful to look to Latin America, the source (via Spain) of Latino culture.

The last section of the book, Latinos in America, looks at how cultural differences affect the behavior and values of Latinos who have come to the United States. Chapters describe what may be distinctive about how Latinos behave as employees of U.S. companies, students in U.S. schools, shoppers in the U.S. marketplace, and as voters in U.S. elections. An additional chapter examines the acculturation of Latinos to U.S. mainstream culture. Like other immigrant groups before them, Latino immigrants differ in the extent to which they have mastered or embraced the mainstream culture of their new country, and this chapter explains how to determine an individual's degree of acculturation to U.S. mainstream culture versus continued adherence to traditional Latino ways.

A repeated theme throughout this book is the complementarity that exists between Latinos and Anglos. While their differences can cause difficulties in working or personal relationships between them, these same differences also enrich their relationships because the strengths and weaknesses of the two groups often complement each other. The coauthors of this book have benefited from this complementarity during their more than 35 years of friendship and collaboration.

Each of the coauthors has also married within his adopted culture. Like Desi Arnaz and Lucille Ball, the Latino author and his Anglo wife have enjoyed a happy, but never dull marriage during their nearly

40 years together. The Anglo author and his Latino wife have been equally happy together, and their marriage of over 30 years has also never been boring. The final chapter of this book discusses the frequent mutual attraction between Anglo women and Latino men, and between Anglo men and Latino women (Latinas), as well as the conflicts their relationships must overcome because of their differences.

PART I

Latino and Anglo Families

CHAPTER ONE

Families

SR:

In my family, my father was el jefe (the boss). My mother deferred to him, and my brothers and sisters and I never questioned his authority. When a decision of importance to the family had to be made, it was my father who made it. Even as a small child, I understood that my father's position in the family did not give him license to do whatever he wanted. I knew that it was also his responsibility to consider my mother's wishes and the wishes and needs of every member of the family when making his decisions.

During my childhood, life in Colombia became increasingly difficult. The country's economy was deteriorating, and political chaos and violence were increasing. As our family struggled with these realities, Los Estados Unidos (the United States) beckoned to us, as it did to many Colombians, as a land of riches, opportunity, and safety.

My father struggled for a long time with the decision of whether we should emigrate to the United States. He believed that my brothers and sisters and I would have a better life in the U.S., and that we would be able to obtain a good education and become successful there. However, in Colombia we had our close and loving extended family, and our grandmother, aunts, uncles, cousins, and godparents were part of the fabric of our daily lives. Without exception, every one of these individuals agreed that we ought to remain in Colombia.

It was not until many years after my father brought us to the United States that I understood how difficult making the decision to emigrate must have been for him. As an adult, I realized how he must have agonized over leaving our family in Colombia, suffered the anger of our relatives for emigrating, and feared that he had failed us by bringing us to the U.S. during the many difficult years we experienced after we arrived.

MI:

When I was ten years old, my parents bought their first new car, a two-tone green 1952 Dodge coupe. They decided that we would take the new car for a summer vacation trip, first to New York City and then Niagara Falls. Like other important family decisions, this one was made jointly by my father and mother, who probably soon forgot whose idea it had originally been.

Once my parents announced their plans, my older brother, younger sister, and I each began vigorously lobbying for our versions of what the trip itinerary should be. Our lobbying continued throughout the entire trip. At times arguing became so heated that my father had to stop the car and threaten to return to Cleveland. We knew he wouldn't, but we also knew that he was angry, so we would call a temporary truce.

I don't remember who was responsible for suggesting each activity, but highlights of that unforgettable trip included going to the top of the Empire State Building, taking a sightseeing boat to the Statue of Liberty, and eating a mysterious concoction that rose several inches on our plates called an "Egg Mountain." Unfortunately, we did not get to don yellow rain slickers at Niagara Falls and board the tourist boat "Maid of the Mist" as I had fervently urged.

The family is the basic unit of every culture, the first and usually the most powerful vehicle for passing cultural values, beliefs, and skills from one generation to the next. Though every culture is organized into family units, the composition and the structure of the family varies from culture to culture. The form the family takes both reflects a culture's core values, as well as shaping those values in the next generation.

La Familia

The typical Latino family is not democratic. Father is the head of the family, mother is the second in command, and children are expected to be obedient and respectful to both of their parents. The Latino family places emphasis on maintaining harmony and avoiding conflict. Open disagreements between family members, which might not be considered inappropriate in an Anglo family, are typically considered confrontational and inappropriate in Latino families.

Most Latino families are also characterized by a high degree of interdependence between family members. Parents are not anxious for their children to grow up too quickly, so independence is not encouraged. Even as adults, most Latino children never move far away from their parents. Until they marry, and sometimes even afterward, many Latino children remain in their parents' homes. Others establish their own homes and raise their families in the same neighborhoods as their parents. Most also remain emotionally dependent on their families in adulthood to a degree not often found in Anglo families.

The Anglo Family

Most Anglo families are more democratic than the typical Latino family, and most Anglo fathers do not function as strong, authoritarian leaders of their families. Among religious conservative groups such as the Promise Keepers (Dowd 1997), some families have attempted to adopt a more authoritarian family structure, with the father designated as the undisputed head of the family. However, these groups must struggle against strong cultural currents. It is more common in Anglo families for fathers and mothers to make decisions jointly, and children are also often allowed a voice in decisions affecting the whole family.

More bickering is tolerated in the typical Anglo family than in Latino families, and so Anglo families are usually good training grounds for learning to compromise. Latino family life, with its emphasis on maintaining harmony, may provide better training in diplomacy and interpersonal sensitivity.

Besides being democratic, the typical Anglo family is also characterized by independence among family members. Independence is encouraged in Anglo children, beginning in infancy, and two-job couples often make the difficult decision to place their infants in childcare when they are only a few months old. Even if a mother chooses to stay at home, she generally weans her baby early compared to mothers in other parts of the world. Infants are encouraged to begin walking and attempts are often made to toilet train toddlers before they have developed the sphincter control necessary to do so. A growing movement in the United States is even advocating a "diaper free" approach from birth, as a way for the child to begin in infancy to learn control of body functions (Ngowi 2007).

¡Un Bebé! (A Baby)

Like most Latino children, Felipe was born into a large, close extended family. As soon as his parents confirmed his mother's pregnancy, they began telling each of the many members of their extended family. Although his parents had only been married for a few months, their relatives had been eagerly awaiting this important news; there had already been speculation about the possibility that the couple was unable to have children.

Felipe's *abuelos* (grandparents), and his many *tías* (aunts), *tíos* (uncles), and *primos* (cousins), as well as family friends were quick to offer the expectant parents support and lots of advice. When he was born, every family member who was able came immediately to see him and to congratulate Felipe's parents, because not doing so would have been considered a failure to fulfill an important family obligation. The church was full for his baptism, which was seen as an important community event, rather than the small family affair it would have been for an Anglo child.

Felipe's family's approach to childrearing was relaxed during his infancy, toddler, and preschool years. His parents were not eager for him to grow up too fast, and behaviors they associated with independence, such as aggressiveness and personal ambition, were discouraged.

Among Latinos, the adjective *ambicioso*, which translates as both "ambitious" and "greedy," is usually used in a negative way. In contrast, being ambitious is considered a positive trait in Anglo culture, and passive children are often urged to be more ambitious in their schools, sports, and other pursuits. Pressures on Latino children tend toward dependence, and this creates strong ties to their families and also to their extended families. As a result, their sense of who they are is provided by their family membership to a much greater degree than that of Anglos, who must define their own identities.

A Blessed Event!

Before Tommy was born, his first-time parents prepared themselves for parenthood by reading books for expectant parents, much as they had prepared themselves for his birth by attending childbirth classes. His mother, a high-school teacher, arranged to take six weeks of maternity leave. She scouted daycare centers until she found one that impressed her as cheerful and well-run and that was willing to provide care for an infant.

It was painful for Tommy's mother to leave her baby for several hours every day, but she and her husband were not prepared to accept the less affluent life-style that would have resulted from the loss of one of their two incomes. Nor was she ready to give up a career she enjoyed, and which had required four years of college to obtain. After she returned to her teaching job, she tried hard to spend quality time with Tommy. She began reading books to him when he was less than six months old, and was pleased that he seemed to pay close attention to all of the pictures.

Tommy's mother and father were excited when he took his first steps and spoke his first words shortly before his first birthday. They worried about him not being toilet-trained by his second birthday until they consulted with a child psychologist, who assured them that the average child is not physiologically ready for toilet training until after 24 months of age. They enrolled him in an academically oriented preschool when he was three years old, and were thrilled when he learned to read before he started kindergarten.

Latino and Anglo families both attempt to provide their children with the love and guidance needed to function successfully in their culture. However, they go about doing so in different ways, consistent with the core values of each group. Differences in childrearing techniques in Latino and Anglo cultures begin to exert their influence on children in each culture almost from the moment of birth. In infancy, the most striking of these differences is in the encouragement or discouragement of independence. As children grow older, differences in family structure and childrearing techniques increasingly differentiate the Latino and Anglo child.

CHAPTER

TWO

Fathers

SR:

When I was twelve, my parochial school had one of the "paper drives" that were popular fundraisers at the time. Like my classmates, I pulled a wagon around my neighborhood, asking my neighbors for their old newspapers. While collecting papers, I made an exciting discovery—some people donated not only old newspapers, but also magazines—and some of those magazines contained pictures of naked women.

I kept those magazines in my room until my mother found them. She said nothing to me, but instead reported the matter to my father. Shortly afterward, my father spoke to me about the magazines. He wasn't angry and he didn't punish me, but he told me that if I wanted the magazines, I needed to keep them in the garage. His message to me was clear: Looking at pictures of naked women wasn't bad, but offending my mother was.

MI:

My happiest memories of my father were of the times (which were infrequent) when I had his undivided attention. My father worked long hours to support our family, and when he was at home, I had to share his attention with my older brother and younger sister, and later with our youngest brother, whose arrival was a surprise to all of us.

Occasionally, my father would be given a complimentary pair of baseball or football tickets at work. My mother and sister had no interest in sports, so my older brother and I took turns accompanying my father to watch the Cleveland Indians or the Cleveland Browns play. I can remember perfectly the excitement I felt climbing the stairs and then entering Cleveland stadium with my dad, and cheering with him when Al Rosen hit a towering home run or Bob Feller struck out another batter with his blazing fastballs; or watching Jim Brown score five touchdowns in one game, each while carrying two or three hapless defenders on his back.

The biological role of fathers is a limited one. While human mothers carry and nourish their children in their wombs from conception to birth, and most are then able to provide their babies with milk produced by their own bodies, a father's biological role in parenthood consists only of providing DNA.

The more central biological role of mothers in producing children is often paralleled by a greater role in childrearing than that of fathers. The roles assigned to fathers vary considerably across cultures, and the behaviors expected of Latino and of Anglo fathers often differ.

El Jefe (The Boss)

Compared to Anglo fathers, Latino fathers typically relate to their sons in a way that is both more formal as well as more affectionate. Their affection is that of a caring mentor. A Latino father does not try to be a "pal" to his son, and he feels no need to justify exercising his authority over his son.

There is considerable emphasis within the Latino family on pleasing the father, rather than on following a standard, preordained set of rules, as is more often the case in Anglo families. Among the few rules that are considered absolute is that the Latino son will treat females and older members of his family with respect, and that he will also insist on respect for his family from those outside the family.

Felipe, like most Latino boys, always addressed his father as sir ("*Si señor*," "*No, Señor*," and so on). Felipe seldom disagreed with his father openly, and never did so in public. He rarely asked his father why he needed to do something requested, as Anglo boys sometimes do with their parents. When he did so, the answer would invariably be "Because I'm your father and I want you to." Felipe was no more obedient than the average Anglo boy, but he did not question his father's authority.

On one occasion during his adolescence, Felipe disobeyed his father when he was told not to attend a friend's party. When it was discovered that he had, in fact, attended the party, a family crisis resulted. What upset his family most was not that he had attended the party, or even that he had sneaked out of his house to do so. It was that he had defied a direct order from his father. On this occasion, even Felipe's older cousin, who was usually his coconspirator in his shenanigans, was upset with him, and told him that he had gone too far.

It is understood that the Latino father will define the limits of acceptable behavior for his son, and that the mother will be responsible on a day-to-day basis for assuring that these limits are honored. When a Latino son misbehaves, it is expected that his mother will deal with the offense, unless it is a serious one.

Serious violations, such as those resulting in suspension from school or involvement with the law, or defiance of a direct order from his father, will trigger his father's involvement, which is likely to be stern and forceful. Unlike the typical Anglo father, the Latino father relies not only on his absolute authority within the family, but also on the manipulation of guilt and shame.

In the case of Felipe's misbehavior, his father pointed out what a disappointment Felipe was to him, and how his behavior was a source of shame, in addition to disturbing the peace and harmony of the family. Coming from his father, these pronouncements were extremely effective and Felipe never repeated his infraction.

A Latino father's orders must be distinguished from his *consejos*, or advice, to his son. Unlike the situation in most Anglo families, where fathers' advice to their sons is seen as nagging or unnecessary lecturing, the *consejos* of Latino fathers are usually seen as valuable advice given by an older, wiser man to a less knowledgeable young person. It is common for Latino boys or even young men to say, *"Mi papá es bueno. Me da muchos consejos."* ("My father is a good father. He gives me lots of advice.")

When Felipe wanted to follow the example of one of his friends who had had his ear pierced, his father called him in, not to demand that he not have his ear pierced, but to offer him *consejos*. He explained to Felipe that there was a biblical prohibition against a man marking his body, and warned him that in his society a boy wearing an earring might be seen as effeminate or rebellious, which could be a disadvantage in many social situations. Felipe considered his father's advice and decided not to have his ear pierced.

In addition to issuing orders and giving *consejos*, Latino fathers communicate in more subtle ways to their sons about what is appropriate behavior. It is in what he does not say, as well as by the example of his own behavior, that the Latino father allows his son to understand the privileges that he may enjoy as a male in his society.

For example, Latino men are given greater license than women to abstain from required religious practices. Most Latino families are Roman Catholic, and the Roman Catholic Church requires that its members attend Sunday Mass, under pain of mortal sin. However, it is more common for Latino mothers to obey this directive along with their daughters and young sons. As the sons grow older, they come to understand that, like their fathers, they are less bound than the women in their family to strictly comply with the directives of the church.

Among the directives of the Catholic Church is a prohibition against premarital sex. Within Latino culture, unmarried women are expected to strictly observe this prohibition. However, unmarried men are allowed considerable freedom to engage in sexual experimentation. Many Latino fathers communicate directly or indirectly to their sons that it is permissible for them to ignore the church's prohibition against premarital sex, and some continue the custom of taking their sons to houses of prostitution for their sexual initiation.

When a Latino son (or much more rarely, a daughter) seriously violates his father's authority, he risks banishment from the family. The grounds for banishment vary from family to family. However, certain actions, like striking his father, or engaging in severely taboo sexual behavior such as homosexuality, are almost universally perceived as justification for banishment.

While in Anglo families there may be periods when parents and children do not speak to each other, these rifts seldom approach the intensity of the estrangement between a Latino father and the child who has defied him. In an Anglo family, parent-child estrangements may be resolved by either parent or child approaching the other and apologizing. In a Latino family, it is the father who determines if, and when, reconciliation may occur.

An elementary school teacher from Guatemala suffered banishment from her family when she defied her father's demand that she stop seeing a U.S. Peace Corps volunteer whom she had met at her school and had begun dating without her parents' permission. Her banishment resulted not from having entered a relationship with this man, but from her having defied her father's directive regarding an issue considered to be of such great importance to her family. She married without the support and participation of her family, and returned with her husband to the United States. It was not until more than three years later, following the birth of her son (her parents' first grandchild) and the intercession of a sympathetic aunt that this young woman and her family were finally reconciled.

Fathers and Sons

Tommy's father was less involved in his day-to-day care than his mother was, even though both had jobs that were equally demanding. Anglo fathers have traditionally had a relatively minor role in childrearing, though men in Tommy's father's generation are spending more time with their children than their fathers did, and some have even taken over the role of househusband and primary caregiver of their children. Their Anglo forefathers were the pioneers who faced the dangers of the frontier while their wives took responsibility for creating a home and raising the children. Most Anglo men today continue to find their identity in their work, rather than within their family life.

The infancy and childhood of most Anglo boys is primarily populated by women. Although his father does share in the excitement of major accomplishments like his first steps or first words, it is generally his mother who is responsible for dealing with his daily care (even if she is also employed), and who cheers his small accomplishments along the road of his development. When he is in daycare, or begins preschool, it is mostly female adults, rather than males, who are in charge of him. The same is true when he attends elementary school. The role of his father and of other men during these years is usually minor compared to the role of his mother.

This was true in Tommy's case. His mother usually changed his diapers when she was at home, put him to bed at night, and read to him. It was also his mother who toilet-trained him, with the assistance of his daycare providers. All of his daycare providers were women, as were his preschool teachers. During his elementary school years, all of his teachers except for Mr. Franklin, his fourth-grade teacher, were women.

For Tommy, the one area of his life in which men played a central role was that of sports. Tommy's father was pleased to help coach his son's baseball teams. By doing so, he was able to encourage Tommy's competitiveness and good sportsmanship, as well as to show him that he wanted to be his friend.

When they play sports together or argue about the relative merits of their favorite teams, the Anglo father and his son are mirroring what Anglo men do together as part of their friendships. Good relationships between fathers and sons are usually buddy relationships, rather than ones based on awe or respect. Anglo boys' role models are more likely to be professional athletes or rock musicians, than their fathers.

Most of the time, the typical Anglo father and his son navigate the waters of childhood comfortably together. However, when conflicts between them do arise, the Anglo father finds himself caught between the dual roles of parent and friend. Many fathers are uncomfortable with setting limits on their sons' behaviors, and they tend to swing between the extremes of setting no limits at all or doing so in an exaggerated way, by taking a "no more Mr. Nice Guy" stance, and Anglo mothers often complain that their husbands' parenting is too extreme.

Tommy's mother felt that her husband's parenting was not consistent. For example, her husband would not refuse to buy Tommy an ice cream cone even if it would ruin his appetite for dinner. On the other hand, when Tommy acted whiny at the end of a long day, his father would become furious with him for being "babyish," and punish him harshly. His mother tried to be both more consistent as well as more understanding with Tommy.

Mi Reina (My Queen)

Within the Latino family, the relationship between father and daughter usually consumes less time than those between father and son, mother and daughter, or mother and son. Nevertheless, the Latino father's relationship with his daughter is crucial to her socialization. While the Latino mother is entrusted with instructing her daughter in the complex and sometimes contradictory role of the Latino female, it is in her relationship with her father that she practices the feminine skills that she is learning.

The birth of Felipe's younger sister, Alícia, was enthusiastically welcomed by her extended family, who hoped that more brothers and sisters would soon follow her and Felipe into the world. Alícia was a beautiful baby, and from the moment she was born, her father doted on her, calling her *mi reina* (my queen). She soon reciprocated her father's affection, and she loved helping her mother to prepare his food and wait on him, serving him his dinner first, before she and her mother and brother sat down to eat together.

Fortunately, Alícia was anxious to please her father, and avoided behaving in any way that would upset him. Her father was extremely proud of her, and wanted her to be present at social events such as *piñatas* (birthday parties), baptisms, and weddings, in order to show the community how feminine and *educada* (well brought up) she was. Like many Latino fathers, Alicia's father felt as if his own character was reflected in the charm, grace, and femininity of his daughter.

The tie between Latino father and daughter does not end when she grows up or marries. Most Anglo families assume that their married daughters will eventually move away, as their husbands' or their own career opportunities dictate. It is expected that the Latino daughter and her husband will live close to her parents and participate in all important family celebrations and events. She is expected to maintain the devotion to her father that her mother instilled in her during her childhood and, in the event of her mother's death or incapacity, it is assumed that the daughter will take over responsibility for her father's well-being.

An example of the devotion toward their fathers which is expected of Latino girls is illustrated by Eugénia, a prominent physician and artist in Mexico City. Eugénia realized at an early age that it pleased her father when she was charming to visitors to their home, danced gracefully, and was attractive to the opposite sex. Growing up in a home with many servants, she helped her mother to ensure that her father was well cared for by their maids, gently scolding them when they were slow or inefficient in serving him.

Eugénia's father appreciated her femininity and charm. He was also somewhat unusual among Latino fathers in being equally pleased by her intellectual and artistic accomplishments. This allowed her to feel confident about her success in school, as well as being gracious and feminine.

When Eugénia followed in her father's footsteps by becoming a physician, she was careful that her achievements complimented, rather than detracted from, his reputation, and she frequently consulted him for professional advice.

As Eugénia's parents aged, she became increasingly attentive to her father's physical and mental needs, even as she maintained her busy career and cared for her own husband and children. During his last illness, she took responsibility for coordinating her father's care, and it was she who made the painful decision to remove life support so that he could die peacefully. Though not all Latino women are as impressively devoted to their fathers as Eugénia, her dutiful behavior is not unusual.

Fathers and Daughters

In most cases, the Anglo father is even less involved in the day-to-day life of his daughter than of his son. He typically defers to the authority of women, including his wife, daycare workers, teachers, and school counselors regarding decisions about his daughter's care. His main role is to delight in his daughter and to be anxious about her development while exercising little control over it.

When Tommy's sister Amy was born, his parents were ready for another child, and they were pleased that she was a girl. His mother again took six weeks of maternity leave, and then arranged for the same daycare provider who had taken good care of Tommy to care for her. Amy's father felt even more inadequate about caring for her than he had with Tommy, and her mother again took major responsibility for her day-to-day care. She continued working full-time at her high school, where she had been promoted to head of the English Department.

Until Amy was about three years old, her mother was the focus of her attention whenever she was at home. When Amy was hungry, bored, or wanted to show off something she had learned, she would seek out her mother. That changed when she discovered that her father was a fascinating creature, very much worthy of her attention.

Amy's parents first noticed this change when she began having occasional nightmares. Since her mother was a heavier sleeper, it was her father who would come and comfort her. After he had checked for monsters under her bed and in her closet, rubbed her back, given her three more hugs and three more kisses, Amy was fortified against all of the world's evils, and could sleep peacefully for the rest of the night.

Concerned about her nightmares, Amy's parents consulted a child psychologist. He wisely suggested that Amy's mother should go in to comfort Amy when she had a nightmare. When her mother appeared after her next nightmare, Amy's response was, "Oh, it's you." She then rolled over and went back to sleep all by herself. After that night, her nightmares ceased to be a problem.

Most little girls don't use Amy's clever way of getting extra attention, hugs, and kisses from their fathers, but most are anxious for his attention between the ages of three and six. The fact that he may be less available than their mothers only makes their fathers more interesting and attractive to them during this stage of their development.

It is generally the Anglo mother who plays the major role in establishing and enforcing rules of conduct for her daughter's childhood and adolescence. This is especially true in the area of sexuality, and it is a rare father who is willing to talk to his daughter about this topic.

This was the case with Amy's father. It was her mother who prepared her for menstruation, and who explained to her why she should take care in dressing as her hips and breasts began developing. The closest Amy's father came to discussing her developing sexuality was to hint to her that males could be dangerous, and that she needed to be "careful" with them. Ironically, Amy and her mother became protective of her father's sensibilities, being careful to never discuss certain topics when he was around.

The role of fathers is an invention of every culture. Within Latino culture, fathers are expected to be the ultimate authority in a close-knit family that emphasizes clear generational boundaries. Fathers are usually less involved in day-to-day childrearing duties, and typically function as loving mentors to their children, insist upon their demonstrating respect for parents, and help to instruct them in appropriate gender roles.

Within Anglo culture, fathers are typically more involved in day-to-day childrearing than their Latino counterparts, are less likely to emphasize generational authority, and usually encourage both independence and gender equality in their children.

Despite the differences in their roles, conscientious Latino and Anglo fathers both seek to provide the love, encouragement, and guidance that are crucial to children growing up to be confident and successful members of their societies.

Mothers

SR:

When I was in sixth grade, I began spending time at the home of my Anglo friend and classmate, Dillard. Many of the customs of his relaxed and informal family seemed strange to me, but none more so than Dillard's calling his parents by their first names. The first time I heard him call his father "Bob," I was shocked. I expected him to be punished for humiliating his father in front of a stranger.

Dillard was not reprimanded for his behavior, and I became intrigued, and then impressed, by my friend's informality with his parents. These feelings lasted only until I made the mistake of imitating Dillard's informality in my own home. When I addressed my mother as "Bertha," I received a disapproving stare and the simple statement "Respetame por favor" (treat me with respect). I did not repeat my mistake.

MI:

Although my father had more formal education than my mother did, it is to my mother that I owe my love of books and the fact that I majored in English as an undergraduate. I can still remember the children's books, like Snipp, Snapp, and Snurr, *and* The Buttered Bread *(Lindman 1995) that she read to my brother and me at bedtime. When my first-grade class began learning to read, I struggled to make the connection between letters, sounds, and meaning until one evening on my mother's lap it all clicked into place as we read a book about penguins together. Suddenly, I could read!*

When I was eight years old, my mother and father decided that it was time for my brother, who was nine, and me to learn about the birds and the bees. It seemed natural that my mother, rather than my father, took on this responsibility, which she accomplished by reading us the book Where do Babies Come From? (Hummel 1994) *I find that I still turn to books whenever I need to learn about something that is new and confusing to me.*

The Yiddish proverb: "God could not be everywhere, so he invented mothers" is one of a myriad of proverbs, legends, and songs from cultures around the world extolling the sacrifices and loyalty of mothers. Since the dawn of the human race, in most cultures mothers have taken major responsibility for shaping the infants they bear into competent members of their societies. How mothers accomplish this difficult task varies across cultures, with each culture, including those of Latinos and Anglos, creating its own variation of the crucial role of mothers.

La Jefa (The Boss Lady)

The typical Latino mother nurtures a strong emotional attachment with both her sons and her daughters. Unlike Anglo husbands, most of whose socializing after marriage is with their wives and other couples, Latino husbands are not expected to stop socializing with their friends after marriage, and they also maintain a strict separation of work and family life. The Latino wife may lack a romantic, emotional relationship with her husband because of his absences, and so she seeks a great deal of emotional closeness with her children. The role of ideal Latino mothers is a self-sacrificing one, and Latino women who take this role to extremes may both smother their children with love and at the same time be overly controlling.

Latino mothers are more likely than Anglo mothers to indulge their children's whims and desires, but also to be stern, strict, and easy to irritate. Most display affection more openly than their Anglo counterparts, but they also demand total obedience. As a result, the Latino child is very concerned about maintaining a good relationship with his or her mother, and is more likely to express love for her openly.

Felipe, as well as his sister Alícia, were anxious to please their mother. This was not difficult for Alicia, who was a quiet and conscientious child. It was considerably more difficult for her boisterous brother Felipe, who was often disobedient. However, he was also an affectionate boy who learned very early how to soften his mother's heart, knowledge that he employed frequently. Not only did his mother invariably forgive his transgressions, but she often helped him to hide his misdeeds from his father.

It is the responsibility of Latino mothers to reinforce for their sons the ideals of machismo. Boys in Latino homes are allowed much greater freedom than their sisters are. As boys grow older, there is less concern about chaperoning their activities, and occasional overuse of alcohol or sexual experimentation is not viewed with the same level of alarm as if they were girls.

Boys are also taught by their mothers that the privileges of Latino maleness bring with them the obligation to behave chivalrously to women, the elderly, and to others who may be weaker than oneself. Boys who do not show appropriate respect for the elderly are reproached. A Latino boy who hits a girl, regardless of the provocation, is similarly reproached.

A Nicaraguan mother living in New Mexico was entertaining friends when her young son struck his female playmate, who had pushed him. The boy's mother drew his attention by quietly calling his name, raising one eyebrow, and saying incredulously: "*¿A una muchacha?*" (You hit a girl?). A Mexican American child tried to explain to his mother that he had hit his sister because she had pinched him. His mother responded: "*¿Tu acaso eres una muchacha?*" (And you are a girl?)

The exception to the rule that the Latino mother is responsible for teaching her sons their appropriate gender role and behavior is the situation in which signs of clearly feminine behavior are seen in boys. Very early in childhood, fathers as well as mothers inform their sons that boys are not to play with dolls, play house, or have any interest in makeup or jewelry. Any signs of femininity in boys are viewed extremely negatively and treated harshly by both parents. A man whose son is seen as feminine is just as likely to be criticized as his wife for their "failure."

An upper-class family in Chile was devastated when their oldest son was killed in an automobile accident. His father took the highly unusual position of accepting his only remaining son's open (though discrete, rather than flamboyant) homosexuality. Because he did not demand that his son reform, or banish the son from the family, the father became the object of considerable gossip in his community and was widely criticized by his neighbors and acquaintances.

Mothers and Sons

The role of the Anglo mother is usually more difficult than that of the Anglo father. During frontier days, she frequently had to function as both nurturer and disciplinarian to her children, and this double role is still evident in many families today. In addition, significant changes over the past century have increased the number of opportunities open to Anglo women for education and career advancement. These changes, while welcomed, have not been an unmixed blessing, because they have further complicated an already challenging maternal role.

Most Anglo women want to have children, but becoming mothers creates conflicts with personal and career goals. Like Tommy and Amy's mother, Anglo mothers often face difficult choices between the demands of their jobs and the desire to spend time with their children. They must also somehow find time for household chores, as well as time to help keep romance alive in their marriages, despite the fact that there are only 24 hours in a day.

Most Anglo mothers feel a special bond with their sons. However, raising their sons is complicated by the fact that while Anglo boys are mostly cared for and directed by women, the women must avoid feminizing them. Like Anglo fathers, Anglo mothers often turn to sports to help make their sons masculine. By signing them up for baseball, football, or soccer teams, as well as for activities like Boy Scouting, mothers gain assurance that their sons are being taught appropriate male social roles within Anglo culture.

Tommy's mother was pleased when her husband became involved in his son's athletic activities. Although she had had little interest in sports herself, she began attending all of Tommy's baseball games, and soon became a knowledgeable baseball fan.

As is often the case in Anglo families, when Tommy entered adolescence, it was his mother, rather than his father, who helped to guide him through the complexities of boy-girl relations. It was his mother who taught him to slow dance, how to ask for a date, and when to buy a corsage.

It was also Tommy's mother's responsibility to determine the limits of her son's acceptable social and sexual behaviors. Ironically, though the Anglo mother lacks the obvious benefit of having been an adolescent male herself, it is generally she, rather than her husband, who struggles with conflicts over dating, appropriate social activities, and sexual experimentation. A mother is expected to allow her son enough freedom to encourage the development of confidence in his sexual identity, while at the same time place limits on him to prevent him from endangering himself or others, hurting his chances for future success, or violating his family's religious and moral code.

When it was time for Tommy to go away to college, his mother would have preferred that he stay at home and attend the local college. Tommy was both excited about the prospect of moving to another city to attend a university as well as anxious about being away from his family and successfully meeting the academic demands of college. His mother felt obligated to hide her desire to keep him close to her, and instead encouraged him to seek a higher quality education out of town. She sometimes wished that she and her husband had not done such a good job of saving money for his education, which would have forced him to attend a local college while living at home. In the end, Tommy did attend a university in another city.

After all of her efforts and the strong bond that she has established with her son, the Anglo mother must accept that he is expected to move away when he is grown. When he marries and starts his own family, his marriage increases the Anglo son's distance from his family, unlike the Latino son, whose wife is expected to help him to maintain his lifelong relationship with his mother.

Jefa e Hija (Daughter)

It is the Latino mother's responsibility to define and enforce the division between masculine and feminine roles and behavior for her daughter. Latino girls who are too rough or who use vulgar language are confronted by their mothers, who demand that their daughters behave in a more feminine fashion. In Anglo society, the challenge to behave in a ladylike way may be seen as old-fashioned. Latino mothers at all socioeconomic and educational levels teach their daughters that certain behaviors are inappropriate for girls simply because they are female.

Alícia's mother, for example, required her to wear dresses or skirts to church, school functions, and social events such as Holy Communion parties and *quinceañeras* (parties celebrating girls' fifteenth birthdays). Her brother Felipe was allowed more leeway in how he dressed for such events. Though Felipe was also allowed to use expressions considered mildly vulgar, such as "*No me friege.*" (Don't bug me) with impunity, Alícia was not.

Had Alícia ignored such instructions in public, her community's reaction would have been strongly negative. For example, if she had attended a party wearing jeans, someone would probably have commented: "*¿Esta niña que? ¿No tiene madre?*" (Doesn't that girl have a mother?)

The feminine role Latino mothers must teach their daughters is complicated. To be feminine in Latino culture is to not only be refined but also to be strong. A Latino woman is expected to be a powerful moral influence within her family. She is also expected to be forceful in defending her family's honor.

A conscientious mother in Colombia was observed securing a place for her five young children at the very front of a large crowd of onlookers at a parade. Whenever anyone tried to push in front, blocking her children's view, she angrily removed them. One of her neighbors, observing this little drama, wryly commented: "*Allí esta la*

Señora Montoya, con su kinder." (There's Mrs. Montoya, with her kindergarten class). Overhearing her, Señora Montoya shot back: *"Daría todo lo que tiene, y mas que no tiene, para tener un kinder así."* (You'd give everything you have, and some that you don't, to have such a kindergarten class). She thus defended her family while subtly insulting her detractor's femininity.

The Latino mother must prepare her daughter to modestly allow her husband to be head of the household, while at the same time she must accept the responsibility for establishing and maintaining the values and structure of the family. The mother-daughter relationship is often complicated by the daughter's resentment against such seeming contradictions in the female role. It is in large part because of the Latino mother's generosity and affection toward her daughter that the daughter is able to endure this complex training.

When the mother-daughter interaction is working well, the daughter reciprocates her mother's generosity and open affection. Mother and daughter help one another enjoy the strength and power of their position and maintain an almost winking acknowledgment of the behind-the-scenes influence of the female role in a well-functioning Latino family.

When the Latino mother-daughter relationship is not working well, the daughter's resentment is directed against her mother, rather than against her father or men in general. Under these circumstances, the relationship may deteriorate to the point where it is characterized by resentment, criticism, and passive aggressive behavior on the part of both mother and daughter.

In many Latino families, especially among the middle and upper classes, grown children assemble for a ritual weekly or monthly meal in their mother's home. The Maldonados, an upper-class family in Monterrey, Mexico, observed this ritual faithfully. Year after year, the family matriarch's four married daughters, along with their spouses, their children, and as they grew up, their children's *novios* (boyfriends) and *novias* (girlfriends) arrived at her home every Sunday after Mass for a luxurious brunch. The matriarch's sons-in-law had long ago given up attending Sunday Mass, but were nonetheless required to attend these ritual meals. Few Monterrey families were so successful at maintaining a tradition like this, and this family was widely admired for doing so.

When the mother-daughter relationship is strained, these ritual meals are a burdensome reminder of the mother's insistent control of her children. When the relationship becomes so uncomfortable that the daughter refuses to return to her mother's home for these meals, the community perceives that both mother and daughter have failed, and both are viewed with a combination of criticism and pity.

This problem existed among the Chávezes, a small family of humble means living on the outskirts of Monterrey, Mexico, who also practiced the ritual of assembling for a weekly meal together. Each Sunday after ten o' clock Mass, the grown children of the family would gather at their parents' home. Because of limited resources, the meal they shared was a simple one, usually consisting only of *empanadas* (deep-fried pastries with meat filling) and coffee. One daughter, whose husband had had a falling-out with his mother-in-law, began absenting herself from these humble weekly gatherings. The result of what would be considered only a minor act of rebelliousness in an Anglo family plunged the Chávezes into crisis, and the daughter's siblings angrily accused her of "ruining" their family with her disrespect toward their mother.

Rarely does the relationship between a Latino mother and daughter become this difficult. It is far more often the case that the ritual of the family assembling for a meal is a reexperiencing of the mother's generosity and her daughter's fidelity, because in most Latino families the relationship between mother and daughter is a rich and continuing source of closeness, comfort, and sharing.

Mothers and Daughters

Raising a daughter is less complicated for the Anglo mother than raising a son. Because her daughter is cared for and supervised primarily by herself and other women, an Anglo mother does not have the same concerns about her daughter's femininity that she has about her son's masculinity. She is comfortable with her daughter's participation in a variety of after-school activities that reflect her own and her daughter's interests, such as music lessons, sports, or Girl Scouts. She also enjoys having her daughter accompany her on shopping trips.

Having grown up accompanying her parents to her brother Tommy's baseball games, Amy's interest in sports developed naturally. When she was eight years old and asked to join a soccer team, her mother was pleased. Because adult volunteers were in short supply, she read books about soccer and volunteered to become an assistant coach for her daughter's team. Both parents were pleased when Amy quickly developed into a star player on her team.

When Amy was in elementary school, she enjoyed shopping with her mother. Amy's mother had excellent taste in clothes, and Amy learned a great deal about style from her mother. While in middle school, Amy began asking permission to go shopping at the mall with her girlfriends, though she continued to shop with her mother for school clothes or whenever she needed to make a more expensive purchase. Amy also began asking her parents to allow her to spend more time on weekends with her friends and to be excused from family activities in order to do this.

While the Anglo daughter usually begins spending more time with her friends and less with her mother once she enters adolescence, most Latino mothers and their adolescent daughters continue to share a broad range of activities. A Latino mother is likely to take her daughter along wherever she goes, including not only on shopping trips, but also to the beauty salon, doctor appointments, and social visits. The amount of time that the typical Latino mother and her adolescent daughter spend together could be considered stifling by most Anglo daughters.

Once her daughter reaches adolescence, an Anglo mother is likely to struggle with the question of how to deal with her daughter's emerging sexuality. Anglo culture does not provide clear guidelines for this, unlike Latino culture, in which an unmarried woman's sexual activity is clearly disapproved of, lowers her value as a potential wife, and reflects badly on her family.

Wanting her daughter to be comfortable with her sexuality, but also anxious to protect her from pregnancy, disease, or exploitation, the Anglo mother attempts to define for her daughter a balance between sexual expression and sexual restraint. Many mothers are willing to tolerate more sexual experimentation on the part of their daughters than they themselves practiced prior to marriage. Like Anglo fathers, they are also often willing to consider current social trends and the opinions of experts regarding their daughters' behavior.

Although Amy's mother believed that it was wrong to have sex before marriage and wanted her daughter to remain a virgin, she was also realistic. As a high-school teacher and a well-read individual, she knew about the high frequency of sexual experimentation among teenage boys and girls, and she worried about her daughter being exposed to both the risk of pregnancy and as the risk of sexually transmitted diseases (including HIV/AIDS). She elected to give Amy a mixed message about sex: Don't have sex, but take these birth control pills, and also be sure to use condoms if you do choose to experiment with sex.

As their relationship grew beyond the struggles over independence and sexual expression that had characterized Amy's adolescence, Amy and her mother began to enjoy the benefits of a richer and more mature relationship. However, there was an undercurrent of sadness. As Amy began preparing to go away to college, both she and her mother understood that this would probably be the last time they would ever live together. Both knew that in all likelihood the demands of career and marriage would eventually take Amy to another community, and perhaps to another state.

Though their emotional separation may be less dramatic than that between herself and her grown sons, the Anglo mother may face limited contact and less opportunity than she would probably prefer for the growth of her relationship with her daughter.

Although she may not be able to be a full-time parent, the Anglo mother shares with the Latino mother, as well as mothers around the world, a devotion to her children that may be unique in human relationships. Unlike the Latino mother, who usually enjoys a lifetime of close interaction with her children, the Anglo mother's most active involvement with her sons and daughters is likely to end when her children marry, if not before. For both parents and children, the independence that Anglos cherish comes at a high price.

CHAPTER FOUR

Becoming an Adult

MI:

High school was a time of preparing to leave home for me. I spent less and less time with my family. I was busy with friends, dates, and part-time jobs, first as a delivery boy for a butcher shop and later as a waiter in a diner. I also made several trips to visit prospective colleges. I felt as if I had been waiting my entire life to get away from Cleveland, and when I was offered a scholarship to attend Northwestern University in Evanston, Illinois, I felt as if my real life was finally going to begin.

I experienced no homesickness during my first year away at school. College life was too exciting for that, with new friends, dates with pretty sorority girls, and Saturday afternoon football games, as well as challenging classes. Visits to my family during school vacations were pleasant, but Cleveland was no longer my home.

In the years after Northwestern, the process of moving away accelerated. I attended graduate school at Berkeley, which was not 400 miles from Cleveland, like Northwestern, but 2,000 miles away, and returned to my parents' home even more infrequently. Then I spent two years as a Peace Corps volunteer in West Africa and later settled and established a family in Guatemala.

Young birds of many species are unceremoniously pushed out of their nests when they reach a certain stage of development. The message from their parents is clear: You are now an adult and must fend for yourself. Becoming an adult in pre-technological human societies also lacked ambiguity; beginning in early childhood, children were taught the skills and knowledge of their tribe, and once they had reached sexual maturity they underwent rites of passage that initiated them into adulthood.

In modern, technological societies such as those in Latin America and the United States, the period between when a child reaches sexual maturity and when he or she has gained sufficient skills and knowledge to survive independently in society is a protracted one known as adolescence. Each modern culture has its own way of treating adolescents and preparing them for adult life, and those ways differ markedly in Latino and Anglo cultures.

Pulling Away—or Not

The extent of the differences between Anglo and Latino approaches to childrearing is nowhere more evident than in adolescence. With the tacit consent of their parents, most Anglo adolescents lead increasingly independent lives, spending relatively little time with their families. They often have after-school jobs, arrange their own entertainment schedules, which usually do not include many recreational activities with their parents, and they may seldom even share a meal with their families.

Within the Latino family, the emotional and physical closeness that exists between parents and their children is maintained during adolescence. This is even evident in the way Latino parents continue to greet their adolescent children with kisses and embraces, something that most Anglo teenagers would not tolerate, even if they did so when younger.

The teenaged children of the Maldonado family of Monterrey, Mexico, whose ritual weekly brunches were described earlier, would always kiss their *abuela* upon entering her home. They would then kiss their mothers and fathers in the presence of the gathered family. Then they would kiss each of their uncles and aunts. This ritual was repeated when they left. In one morning, these adolescents would kiss more family members than most Anglo teenagers do in a year.

Adolescence in Latino culture, like adolescence in Anglo culture, is a time of rebellion and experimentation. However, most Latino teenagers are considerably less defiant of parental wishes and norms than their Anglo counterparts. While Anglo adolescents expect and tolerate only minimal intervention in their lives, Latino adolescents accept that their parents' wishes will be a crucial determinant of all that they do.

But Those Are My Friends!

Latino parents' involvement in the lives of their adolescent children includes exerting control over their children's choice of friends. Latino adolescents want their parents to approve of their friends, and they understand that if their parents truly disapprove, they are likely to be prohibited from seeing these friends. Latino parents also insist on knowing, or at least knowing about, the parents of their friends, so that they can judge whether their children are associating with *buena gente* (people who are of good families), or not.

This was true of the daughters and sons-in-law of Señora Maldonado. Even Carlos, the most cosmopolitan of her sons-in-law, who ran a large import-export business, traveled extensively in the United States and was eager for his children to attend college there, insisted on getting to know all of his sons' and daughters' friends. Carlos always took the time to talk to his children's friends about their activities when they came to the house, and he always asked them to convey his greetings to their parents.

On one occasion, Carlos refused to let his eldest son associate with a classmate from an even wealthier family, whom he knew to be involved in illegal activities, stating, "*La família de Ricardo no me caye bien*" (literally, "I can't stomach Ricardo's family"). However, he had no objections to his daughter befriending a girl from a humble family, since he knew of her father, who was a hard-working, honest man.

Most Anglo parents do not insist on getting to know all of their adolescent children's friends, and they are considerably less likely than Latino parents to dictate who their children's friends will be. Although they may feel uncomfortable with their sons' or daughters' choices of companions, Anglo parents will usually not forbid their children to associate with someone, unless they believe that that individual is influencing their child to neglect schoolwork, use drugs, or otherwise break the law. Most Anglo parents understand that if they attempt to control their adolescent children's friendships, they run the risk of precipitating a full-scale rebellion, with more dramatic deterioration in behavior resulting.

The reaction of Elizabeth's parents, who were already participating in family therapy for other issues, was typical. On entering high school, Elizabeth started hanging out with a group of classmates who dyed their hair primary colors, wore black, and sported body piercings and tattoos. When her parents raised objections about her choice of friends, she announced that she was going to continue to associate with her new friends, no matter what her parents said. Because she continued to earn good grades and they felt confident that she was not experimenting with drugs, Elizabeth's parents reluctantly decided to back down. By not forbidding Elizabeth to see her new friends, they avoided an all-out confrontation with their daughter.

Dates versus *Novios*

Though Latino parents are often intrusive regarding their children's friendships, they are even more so when it comes to their adolescent children's dating relationships. Anglo parents may at times raise objections about who their children date (often along racial or religious lines), but if they do so there is considerable risk that their children will defy them and continue to see that individual, either openly or secretly.

Latino adolescents, as well as unmarried adults, are permitted much less freedom about whom they date than Anglo adolescents. The dating relationship, or *noviazgo*, is more formal in Latino culture, which traditionally requires the consent of the parents of the *novia*. Most Latino parents will forbid their daughter to have a relationship with a *novio* who is not "*de nuestra clase*" (of our socioeconomic class), or whose parents they do not consider to be *buena gente*. Most Latino parents will also impose the same restrictions on their son's choice of a *novia*.

MI:

My courtship of my wife, Colombina, was very much influenced by her family's insistence on approving of her boyfriends. Our romance began after the Guatemalan earthquake of 1976, when nearly 30,000 people were killed and whole villages were left homeless. Both of us were employed by the Institute of Nutrition of Central America and Panama (INCAP), a World Health Organization research institute, and we met while on a rescue mission to villages destroyed by the earthquake.

Our budding romance was complicated by the fact that Colombina already had a novio, *a young banker approved of and much esteemed by her family. A master of her culture, Colombina insisted on keeping our relationship from all but a few trusted friends for several uncomfortable months, while she broke off with her persistent* novio *and carefully prepared her family for the shock of that breakup and the even greater shock of her being in love with an Anglo.*

Before Colombina's family would allow her to become my novia, *I was required to arrive, with my parents, at her home in a mountain province of Guatemala, pass muster, and formally request that I be permitted to court her. My parents, who had visited Guatemala the previous year, were unable to return. Instead I presented myself with a distinguished Guatemalan anthropologist colleague and his wife, who were able to vouch both for me and for my family, whom they had met on their earlier visit to Guatemala.*

I can recall few details of my interview with Colombina's family, but I do remember it being at least as stressful as my doctoral oral exam. However, once I had received their approval, Colombina's family treated me with warmth and kindness, and they have made me feel like a valued member of their family ever since.

In part, the demand for control by parents over their children's dating partners is a natural consequence of the fact that the eventual spouse of a Latino son or daughter will become integrated into the family to a much greater degree than is common among Anglos. When Anglos say to the parents of a child about to marry, "Don't think of it as losing a daughter (or son), think of it as gaining a son (or daughter)," they are largely articulating a wish that is destined to be unfulfilled. When an Anglo child marries, it usually reduces close involvement with their family of origin. By contrast, when a Latino son or daughter marries, they not only remain an integral part of their own family, but also become an active part of their spouse's family as well.

First Jobs

Obtaining a first job is considered an important rite of passage for Anglo teenagers. Anglo parents will generally refrain from interfering with their children's employment, unless the job is illegal, dangerous, or interferes with their children's schooling. Wealthy Anglo parents will usually tolerate and often encourage their teenagers to work at menial jobs.

This was true of a wealthy physician father and interior designer mother of a 17-year-old boy, who sought family counseling, listing as one of their concerns the fact that their son had never worked. The counseling went well, and when their son obtained a job working for a janitorial service, his parents were delighted. His father expressed the opinion that this job would teach his son how hard it was to make money, as well as give his son respect for menial labor.

Latino parents often view their children's employment quite differently. They are likely to restrict their teenage children's employment if they feel that a job is not in keeping with the status or dignity of their family.

SR:

When I was in high school, I wanted to get a job, like most of my friends, and save money for college. I was fortunate enough to get hired as a busboy at a prestigious New Orleans restaurant, Antoine's. I was proud of having a job, especially in a famous restaurant. My parents knew that my friends worked, and that I needed money for my education, so they did not oppose my employment. However, my relatives in Colombia were outraged that my family would allow me to work in a restaurant, a job considered low class and disreputable.

To my Colombian family, women who worked in restaurants were considered "loose," and men were suspected of being homosexuals. By allowing me to work in a restaurant, my family believed that my parents were allowing me to associate with people who were decidedly not buena gente, *thus lowering the status of our family.*

I kept my job at Antoine's but it was at the expense of continued reproaches directed toward my mother, and criticism of my father, who was viewed as further compounding his sin of taking us away from the family in Colombia.

When adolescence ends, Latino parents often choose their children's careers, a practice that is rare in Anglo families. If their parents' choice of careers differs from their own, young Latinos must find a way to resolve this disparity. If their parents have raised them as *buena gente*, they will make every effort at resolution without threatening the bonds of love and respect that link them to their families.

The dilemma of wanting a career that was not acceptable to his parents was one which faced the eldest son of a family in Guadalajara, Mexico. The son wanted to be a race car driver. His family was well-to-do, and they were pleased to support his racing, at which he excelled, as a hobby. However, his parents raised vehement objections to his making racing his profession.

The disagreement between the son and his family was so troubling that they sought professional help from a psychologist. With his assistance, the family was able to resolve their conflict and the parents enabled their son to open a copying business that required little of his time. He thus became an entrepreneur, considered a high-status profession, who also raced cars.

Unlike Latino parents, Anglo parents usually allow their children to choose their own careers and seldom oppose their choices. Successfully socialized Anglos seek to be economically as well as emotionally independent of their families as soon as they are able, unlike successfully socialized Latinos, who usually remain more closely involved with their families throughout their lives. Lacking both the obligations as well as the security of the close family ties that characterize Latinos, Anglo young adults are freer to pursue opportunity wherever it calls them. In each culture, "good" families produce the kinds of adults that their culture values.

PART II

Latino-Anglo Cultural Differences

CHAPTER FIVE

Male and Female Gender Roles

SR:

The first time I remember hearing the word macho was from my abuela.
*I was seven or eight years old at the time, and had been wrestling with
my sister Dina, who was my equal in size, strength, and meanness. My*
abuela *called me aside so as not to shame me in front of my sister.*

*She told me that I must never be rough with women (though my
sister was only a girl, rather than a woman), and that I must let them
have the advantage. She concluded with an injunction:* "Uno tiene que
ser macho," *which means literally* "One must be male," *but I understood that she was talking about the profound responsibility of men to
be the protectors and guardians of women, as well as children, and
those who are helpless.*

*That message had been communicated to me in different ways
before that time, but with my* abuela's *injunction to be macho, I finally
understood what it meant to be a Latino man. So, many years after my*
abuela *spoke to me, I still cringe when I hear the term "macho" used to
describe male behavior that is the exact opposite of how she instructed
me to behave toward women.*

My abuela's *message was repeated by my family throughout my
childhood and adolescence, and since we were living in the United
States, I came to understand the differences between the meaning of
gender in my culture and its meaning for Anglos. On one occasion
when I was in high school, I informed my mother that I was going to*

the movies with a girl classmate. None of my classmates had much money, and it was the custom among them for boys and girls to each pay their own way at the movies.

My mother thoughtfully checked to see if I had enough money, and offered to give me more. I explained that I had plenty, because my date and I were each going to pay our own way. As firmly as had my abuela several years before, she informed me, "Un caballero nunca deja pagar a una dama" (A gentleman never allows a lady to pay).

In addition to extending my understanding of the ideals of machismo, my mother was reminding me that even though I had lived longer in the United States than in Colombia, she expected me to live my life according to Latino values. I understood that no matter how Americanized I became, I would always be Latino.

MI:

Although many of the Anglos I knew in Guatemala adapted very well to Latino culture, one of my coworkers at the Institute of Nutrition of Central America and Panama did not. She continually butted heads with several of our Latin American scientific colleagues, who appeared to enjoy annoying her. Outspoken in her feminist views, the more that this woman demanded respect from her male Latino coworkers, the less she seemed to receive.

In contrast, most of the Latino professional women I met in Guatemala seemed to command respect effortlessly. Through a mysterious amalgam of professionalism and femininity, these women were able to increase their effectiveness on the job by adding the deference due them as Latino women to the respect due them as professionals.

In the Book of Genesis, when Adam and Eve ate the forbidden fruit of the tree of knowledge and saw that they were naked, they did not cover their offending eyes, hands, or mouths. They covered their genitalia. The differences between the sexes, both physical and social, have always been a source of fascination and conflict for people throughout the world.

Sex or Gender?

Nature provides the physical differences between men and women, but cultures define the social roles each is expected to play. Bearing children and breastfeeding them limit women's mobility. As a result, cultures have traditionally assigned tasks that require being away from home for long periods such as hunting, whaling, and fighting wars, to men, and tasks which are performed close to home and can be easily interrupted, such as cultivation of crops or foraging for food, to women.

However, the tasks assigned to men and women, as well as the behaviors expected of them by their cultures, often have little or nothing to do with the biological differences between them. In Latin America, for example, it is considered unseemly for a man to sweep, wash clothes, or do dishes, and equally unseemly for a woman to repair automobiles, even though having male or female genitalia or secondary sexual characteristics does not help or hinder anyone in performing these tasks.

The arbitrary assignment of tasks based on gender is not confined to Latino culture. Only 2½ percent of Fortune 500 companies have a female CEO (Dickler 2007) and, until 2007, when Harvard chose Drew Gilpin Faust as president, a woman had never led one of the upper echelons of U.S. universities. Until fairly recently, there were many more male than female lawyers, physicians, and engineers, and relatively few male nurses or elementary school teachers.

Rapid changes in conceptions of gender roles are occurring in U.S. society. Many more women are entering traditionally male occupations and more men are entering traditionally female occupations. It was not until the first decade of the twenty-first century that the United States had a female leader of a House of Congress or a female contender in a presidential race.

Changes are also occurring in the behaviors expected of men and women in the United States. In the past, Anglo women often greeted one another by hugging, while men greeted one another with a handshake. Now many Anglo men hug each other when meeting or saying goodbye, though this demonstrativeness is still rare in some parts of the U.S., such as the rural Midwest.

Changes in conceptions of gender roles are also occurring in Latin America, although the process has been a slower one there. Some of these changes, like the fact that dress restrictions on girls and young women imposed by their families are being relaxed, seem less far reaching in their effects, while others, such as the fact that more women are entering the fields of law, politics, and engineering, are clearly of great importance.

Machismo versus Title IX

Despite the fact that changes have occurred in Latin America as well as the United States in the way gender roles are defined, Anglo and Latino cultures continue to differ markedly in how gender roles are viewed in the two cultures. There are many more rules and guidelines governing male and female Latino behavior than for Anglos. Gender role expectations and prerogatives are generally viewed as bias and discrimination in the U.S., but this is not true in Latin America.

In the United States, a majority of women and men have supported a far-reaching, but still continuing, campaign to break down economic, occupational, and educational barriers based on gender. Even in activities where sex differences in size and physical strength are significant, such as playing on high-school football teams, women have successfully petitioned to be allowed to participate.

Within Latino culture, it would be considered bizarre for a girl to ask to play on a boys' sports team. Latino girls and young women participate enthusiastically in sports such as basketball, though always on women-only teams, and it is not competitiveness that differentiates Anglo from Latino girls, but a greater willingness to compete against boys.

MI:

After more than twenty years of living here and becoming acculturated to the United States, my wife Colombina one day surprised me by challenging my son and two other members of his high-school basketball team to a friendly game of HORSE, in which each player must repeat the previous player's successful shot, getting a letter each time they are unable to do so, until they are a HORSE and eliminated. She shocked them by beating all three.

I knew what they were in for. In high school, Colombina had starred on the Guatemalan national scholastic champion team. I had been in her hometown of Santa Cruz del Quiché, where women's basketball is so popular that more than half the town often turns out for routine games. During a holiday tournament, a sixteen-year-old high-school girl who had been the top scorer for the winning team was asked by a local radio announcer what her goals were. Her reply was, "I would like to be another Colombina Rodríguez." Since Colombina's triumph had happened twelve years earlier, the girl was four years old at the time.

The behavior expected of men and of women in Latino culture is well defined. Latino women are expected to be attractive and nurturing, while men are expected to be macho and virile, as well as chivalrous and respectful toward women, those in positions of authority, and the elderly.

Anglo men and women have less clearly defined behavioral expectations. However, Anglo women often demonstrate greater social adeptness and place a higher priority on maintaining good relationships with others than do Anglo men, who may be more likely to define themselves through their jobs than through their relationships or their families. However, these gender differences are dissolving as more young women get on the career fast track and more young men embrace sensitivity and take over greater responsibility for the care of their children.

A Double Standard

In addition to being attractive and nurturing, Latino women are also expected to be virtuous. The double standard is alive and well in Latin America. Unmarried women who have sex are condemned and are considered by many families to be inappropriate wives for their sons.

On the other hand, young Latino men are expected to experiment sexually.

Though it is considered immoral and is not encouraged, many Latino men of the middle and upper classes also have sexual relationships outside of their marriages. They are generally able to safely do so without endangering either their marriages or their reputations in the community.

> *SR:*
>
> *As an innocent teenager, I was shocked to learn that among my many uncles in Medellín, Colombia, were some who maintained relationships with queridas (mistresses). It was even more surprising to me that these uncles were not criticized by members of our family for doing so.*
>
> *When one of my uncles became involved in an extramarital affair that was more intense and more public than is usually accepted in Medellín, his wife approached her mother-in-law in desperation to request her support and assistance. My grandmother's response was, "He's your husband, and if you were doing what you should, he would not look for other women," thus placing the responsibility for my uncle's behavior solely on his wife.*

Latino women are not only expected to be responsible for their husbands' fidelity, but to be themselves always faithful to their own marriage vows.

> *MI:*
>
> *A young woman in my wife's small town of Santa Cruz del Quiché, Guatemala, was considered extremely fortunate when she married a local professional from a well-to-do family. Unfortunately, he turned out to be something less than the great catch he initially appeared to be. Not long after their marriage, he began drinking heavily, spending very little time with his young wife, and not even attempting to hide the several affairs he was conducting.*
>
> *His unhappy wife responded to this treatment by herself beginning an illicit affair. It is difficult to keep adultery a secret in a small Guatemalan town, and her affair was soon both public knowledge and*

a major scandal. While her husband's behavior was considered unfor-
tunate but not remarkable, she was condemned by the town as a scarlet
woman, an immoral person, and a disgrace to her community.

Among Anglos, premarital sex on the part of both men and women is common, though discouraged by parents, religious organizations, and even advertising campaigns urging sexual abstinence before marriage. Extramarital affairs are somewhat less common, though hardly unusual, and in Anglo culture, unlike Latino culture, the discovery of an extramarital affair by either husband or wife is considered grounds for divorce.

Within Latino culture, expectations about what is appropriate or acceptable behavior for men and for women differ dramatically in other areas aside from sexuality. A double standard also exists regarding aggressive behavior. Although (physical) fighting is not encouraged, it is considered far more acceptable for men than for women. More so than among Anglos, women fighting is viewed with disdain and condemnation and beneath their dignity as women.

It is also much more socially unacceptable for Latino women than men to get drunk, and especially publicly drunk, although drinking to excess is not more socially acceptable for Anglo men than it is for Anglo women.

SR:

My sister Dina was raised primarily in the United States, but returned to live in Medellín, Colombia, during her adolescence. Her readjust-ment to Latin America, and particularly to the social restrictions placed on young women, was at times a difficult one.

On one occasion, Dina traveled to a neighboring town with a group of our male cousins, where they attended a party. When they returned home, our cousins reported that they had gotten drunk at the party. This news was received by family members with joking and teasing. However, when Dina confided that she had also gotten drunk, the family was scandalized, and she was soundly reproached. Our relatives would have probably been less upset if she had said, "Estaba copetona" (literally, "I was in my cups"), which is a more dainty and ladylike expression.

Eating to excess, like drinking to excess, is also viewed differently for men than for women in Latino culture. There is little fuss made about men being gluttonous, and doing so is generally seen as an indication of a lusty embrace of life. Latino women, on the other hand, are expected to be more circumspect, and overeating in women is seen as indelicate or unfeminine.

The same sex distinction is also made in Anglo culture, though to a markedly lesser degree. During the second half of the twentieth century, the prohibition against female gluttony was stronger, and Anglo women would sometimes eat at home before going out on a dinner date so that they would be seen by their dates as "eating like a bird" (despite the fact that birds are actually among the most gluttonous of animals).

As is the case with other behavioral expectations, the expectations regarding appropriate behavior for men and for women in their roles as spouses, parents, and children are also generally more explicit and rigid in Latino culture than in Anglo culture.

A Latino husband is the designated head of his family, and he is expected to make all of the significant decisions affecting the family. While her husband is the head of the family, the Latino wife wields considerable power behind the scenes, and her husband is expected to always demonstrate respect for her, and to anticipate her wishes by making decisions which will please her. Latinos often joke that the husband is the *cabeza* (head) of the family, but his wife is the *nuca* (neck), which turns the head.

Role assignments and expectations are murkier in the typical Anglo family. No one is clearly in charge, and decisions affecting the family are generally made jointly, and sometimes after a good deal of conflict, by husbands and wives.

Parental roles are also more clearly delineated in Latino culture than in Anglo culture. Latino mothers act as second in command to their husbands, and are responsible for the day-to-day disciplining of their children. When they are unable to control their children's behavior, they call on their husbands for assistance, and when father steps in, he must be obeyed or the consequences to his children are likely to be dire ones.

Within Anglo culture, mothers have also traditionally assumed the role of day-to-day disciplinarian for their children, but they have had less assurance than Latino mothers that their husbands would step in to back them up when their efforts failed. The role of the Anglo mother is changing, though, as fathers become more directly involved in childcare and women become more involved in their own careers. However, Anglo mothers typically continue to bear the major responsibility for defining the limits of appropriate sexual behavior for both their sons and their daughters.

The influence of gender on the behavior expected of children is also more pronounced in Latino than in Anglo culture. Latino boys are generally forgiven for using rough language or getting into fights, and they are permitted a good deal of leeway regarding sexual experimentation during adolescence. Latino girls are taught from a young age to assist in serving their fathers and brothers. They are expected to be graceful and charming, and any roughness or vulgarity on their part is strongly discouraged. Sexual experimentation by unmarried Latino young women is strictly forbidden.

By contrast, within Anglo culture gender differences in children are increasingly being de-emphasized. Boys are often encouraged to be sensitive rather than rough, and girls are urged by their parents to aspire to do anything that men do.

Anglo and Latino children grow up with very different beliefs about how men and women should behave. As adults, each group strives to live up to the ideals taught to them as children. Anglo men and women both aspire to independence and achievement. Latino women cultivate their femininity, nurturing ability, and attractiveness, while Latino men emphasize their machismo, strength, and virility.

Even feminism has a different meaning in Latino than in Anglo culture. It comes as a surprise to many Anglos that the feminist movement has had a significant impact in Latin America. However, Latino feminists, unlike Anglo feminists, have not focused on equality of opportunity, but on the plight of women having to work for near-slave wages or who are being forced by economic circumstances into prostitution. The Latino feminists' message, consistent with their pride in their femininity, has not been "shame on you for not treating us the same," but "shame on you for not respecting us as women."

Friendship

SR:

When I was in the sixth grade, my best friend was my classmate Dillard, who had so impressed me earlier by calling his father by his first name. He and I hung out together during every recess, ate lunch together in the cafeteria, and after school we spent hours together at each other's houses.

I don't remember what started it, but one day Dillard and I had a falling out at school, and we began fighting on the playground. I was losing, until my tough big brother Al told me, "Bite his ear." I did, and Dillard ran off crying, making me an instant hero to my classmates.

Dillard tried more than once to make up with me, but I refused. Then his younger sister, who also attended our parochial school, died, and they held a Mass for her at school. Dillard's mother approached me at the Mass, and asked me to come and sit with Dillard and their family. Much to my later shame and regret, I stubbornly refused to do so.

When I got home, my mother, who had heard about my refusal from my brothers and sisters, took me aside. More forcefully than she had ever spoken to me about anything, she told me: "¡Nunca, nunca, nunca trata a un amigo asi!" (Never, never, never treat a friend like that!).

My mother is now in her 90s and she has forgotten almost everything, including what country she lives in and that she is a widow. One of the last things she forgot was asking about how each of my friends was doing.

MI:

When I attended Boulevard Elementary School, my best friend Stanley lived on the next block. We spent every day after school and all day long in the summers talking, reading comic books, or exploring the streets on our bicycles. Then my parents bought a bigger house in a nicer neighborhood, and we moved across town. I attended a different school, lost touch with Stanley, and never saw him again.

It was hard for me to make friends at my new school, and I had a lonely sixth grade. Seventh grade was much better. Thirteen boys from my junior high school class, including myself, decided to form a club, which we named the "Aces." We had silver pendants made with "Aces" on the front, and our names engraved on the back, and proudly wore them to school. My friend Mickey's father built us a clubhouse in his backyard where we held meetings and had sleepovers. I have no idea what became of the other members of the Aces, though I did recently learn that Mickey had been elected mayor of his small town in Colorado.

In high school, my best friend Steve and I got our driver's licenses within a few weeks of each other, double-dated, studied, and filled out college applications together. He went to Kent State University in Ohio, and I went off to Northwestern, in Illinois. Steve and I kept in touch during our college years, occasionally visited each other's campuses, and hung out together during summer breaks in Cleveland. Now we talk on the phone once a year or less.

My friend Rick and I were fraternity brothers and college roommates at Northwestern. During the summer before our senior year we both got jobs as waiters in a resort in South Haven, Michigan. That summer, we romanced town girls, slept little, and both made the decision to become psychologists. As had happened with many previous friendships, I lost touch with Rick after he entered graduate school at Penn State and I went to Berkeley.

Last year, I was reading a Newsweek *magazine in a doctor's office waiting room when I came across Rick's name in an article about an organization he had founded to produce school curricula designed to foster the ethical development of children. I contacted him on the Internet, and we resumed our friendship, learning that our lives had often followed uncannily similar paths. Yet, despite our closeness in college, our similar likes and dislikes, and even our identical choice of professions, we had allowed our friendship to languish for more than thirty years.*

The Fragility of Friendships

From David and Jonathan's friendship described in the Old Testament, to that of TV's *Friends*, the value of friendship has been extolled throughout history, and in every culture. Though the desire to have friends may be universal, friendship is the most fragile of human relationships. Unlike most other relationships, such as those between husband and wife, parent and child, or employer and employee, there are no legal or spiritual sanctions that bind one friend to another.

Husbands and wives are bound together both by legal and spiritual contracts. Church wedding ceremonies make each member of the congregation a witness to the marriage being performed. Quaker weddings even underscore the witnessing by the congregation by having everyone present at the wedding sign the marriage certificate. Many marriages do not last "till death do us part," but husbands and wives who wish to end their marriages are required to petition the State for a divorce. They must also face the disillusionment of their families and friends, as well as their religious communities.

Parent-child relationships are even more difficult to destroy. Laws safeguarding the sanctity of the parent-child bond require proof of abuse or neglect in order for the State to terminate parental rights. Laws make it equally difficult for children to emancipate themselves from their parents, or for parents to abrogate their responsibilities, and punish parents for failing to carry out their responsibilities to their children adequately.

Employer-employee relationships, like those between lawyers and their clients, doctors and their patients, and landlords and their tenants, are also regulated by law. Laws governing relationships between employers and their employees have been written because of the necessity for maintaining the stability of these relationships; employers cannot succeed in business without a productive and stable workforce any more than employees can survive without a secure income.

Unlike friendships, husband-wife, parent-child, and employer-employee and other business relationships are protected by formal procedures and laws governing how they begin, are conducted, and end. Friendships have no such formal guidelines or sanctions, and they tend to be the most unstable of all our relationships. We keep the same mother and father throughout our lives, and many remain married to the same spouse throughout their adulthoods. Even employment is often longer-lasting than friendship. Most of the friendships we have made in our lives have been lost.

¡Mi Amigo! (My Friend)

From infancy, Latino children are taught the importance of interdependence and close, harmonious relationships with others, and the results of this training can be seen in the value Latinos place on friendship. Although the practice is discouraged and often illegal in U.S. culture, Latinos openly favor their friends in hiring and promotion decisions and use their influence to assist their friends who must make an appeal to government bureaucrats.

Latinos also include their friends in a wide variety of family events and rituals. While Thanksgiving dinner may be the only family ritual in which many Anglos include friends, Latinos typically invite new and old friends to their children's baptisms, Holy Communions, birthday parties (also known as *piñatas*), and *quinceañeras.*

> **MI:**
>
> *My wife Colombina began a novel and popular trend when we moved to New Mexico, into one of the few communities in the state with relatively few Latinos. For each of our two children's birthdays, she invited not only our children's playmates, but also their parents and other adult friends as well. While the children played, attacked a paper mache piñata full of candy with a broom, and chased each other around with cascarones, or eggshells full of confetti, the adults, most of*

whose only previous contact with other people's children's birthday parties had been to drop off and pick up their kids, ate, relaxed, and socialized.

One way in which the desire for friends is demonstrated in Latino culture is in the creation of a special category of relationships that is not recognized in Anglo culture. This is *tocayo*, a term used to refer to another person with the same first name as yours. As an icebreaker and to encourage friendship you may call anyone with the same first name *tocayo*, a way of establishing an instant bond with them.

Godfathers and Godmothers

Latino culture has also developed a more formal way of maintaining stable, close relationships of friendship and mutual assistance. This happens through the institution of *compradrazgo* (godfatherhood or godmotherhood). By inviting a person to become the *padrino* (godfather) or *madrina* (godmother), or sponsor of their child's baptism and confirmation, Latinos establish an enduring bond with that individual.

> *SR:*
>
> *Two of my students at the University where I teach, a Latina from Mexico and an Anglo, met and married during their graduate studies. When their son was born, they named him "Samuelito" (little Samuel), and asked me to be his padrino, or godfather. As his godfather, it was my responsibility to request of the Catholic Church for him the sacrament of baptism, and to renounce Satan on Samuelito's behalf. When he was thirteen years old, it was also my responsibility to act as sponsor of his confirmation in the Catholic Church.*
>
> *My involvement in my godson's life also extended beyond religious duties. Over the years, both he and his parents have sought my advice and assistance. When Samuelito felt that his parents were pressuring him too much to get good grades, he came to me for help in getting them off his back. When they in turn felt that Samuelito was making his part-time job a higher priority than his homework, his parents*

asked me to talk to him about this. Samuelito is now eighteen and he is in the process of applying to colleges. He has asked me to read over his college application essays.

I have been a part of Samuelito's life since he was born, and we have developed a relationship that has brought me much satisfaction. The friendship that has developed between Samuelito's parents and me has also become a deep and rewarding one. When his mother was diagnosed with cancer, my friends asked me to be with them when they met with her surgeon and he explained the risks and benefits of operating, as well as when they later celebrated her recovery. In thirty-five years of college teaching I have become friends with many of my former students. However, none of these relationships has approached the depth and richness of the one my godson's parents and I have maintained.

When you become a child's *padrino* or *madrina*, a lifelong bond is established between you and your *ahijado* (godson) or *ahijada* (god-daughter). It is the responsibility of the godparents to request the sacrament of baptism for their godchild, and to assure that proper religious training is provided in the event that his or her parents cannot or will not do so. As a godparent, you are not obliged to provide for your godchild's material needs. However, there is an expectation that you will look out for the interests of your godchild, who is in turn expected to treat you with the respect and consideration due a second mother or father.

You and the child's parents become *compadres*, which literally means "parents with," or "co-parents." Whenever you meet, you greet each other as *compadre*, or *comadre*, rather than by name, and you introduce them to others (and they you) as your compadre or comadre. *Compadres* and *comadres* are expected to include one another in celebrations and fiestas and to remember each other's birthdays, as well as at Christmas and other holidays.

Becoming *compadres* or *comadres* is a gratifying way to add stability and permanence to a friendship, as well as to extend social bonds beyond the narrow confines of the family. *Compadre* and *comadre* relationships assure that even if you change jobs or move out of your neighborhood, important friendships will not be lost because they depended heavily on proximity.

These relationships are so popular among Latinos that even individuals who have no children to baptize or confirm will often nevertheless begin referring to a valued friend as *compadre* or *comadre*. By doing this, they indicate their desire for a close and enduring friendship, even though they are unable to establish a formal *compadrazgo* relationship.

You're So Far Away

Anglos value friendship as much as Latinos, but they must overcome greater obstacles to friendship than those in Latino culture, and they lack any formal structure for stabilizing friendships, such as the *compadrazgo* system. Within the United States, some religious organizations, such as the Roman Catholic Church, do utilize godparents. However, the godparent role, even among Catholics, is a very limited one in comparison with the one found in Latin America.

Among Anglos, godparents play a ritual role at the time of baptism. They are almost never involved in the subsequent religious training of their godchildren, and they seldom maintain the meaningful and enduring relationship with their godchildren or their godchildren's parents enjoyed by Latino *padrinos* and *madrinas*. The English language does not even have a word, such as *compadre*, to describe the relationship between godparents and their godchildren's parents.

Not only does Anglo culture lack any formal structure for stabilizing friendships, but maintaining friendships is made more difficult for Anglos by the mobility that characterizes people's lives in the United States. According to the U.S. Census Bureau, over forty million Americans change residences every year (Schecter 2004), and most Anglos live someplace far from where they were born.

By contrast, most people in Latin America remain in the same community throughout their lives and often in the same neighborhood where they were born. In recent decades, many Latinos have been forced to relocate from their rural communities to urban centers or to emigrate to the United States because of political upheavals or economic hardship. They have typically moved into *barrios* (neighborhoods) where relatives, *compadres*, or friends have previously located, often moving in with these individuals until they were able to find their own housing nearby. In the past, Irish, Italian, Jewish, and other ethnic groups migrating to the U.S. did the same.

For Anglos today, the decision of where to live is seldom based upon the fact that friends or relatives have previously moved to a place. Priority is more often placed on the opportunity for economic and social advancement offered by a location.

MI:

When my wife Colombina and I moved to northwestern New Mexico in 1981, this area, which is rich in oil, gas, and coal reserves, was in the middle of an economic boom. We met many others who had come to our community to work in the oil and gas industry or the two nearby coal-fired power plants, or to serve the families of those who did as doctors, lawyers, teachers, merchants, and psychologists. Recent arrivals easily outnumbered those who had been born here. While we have stayed and raised our children in the community, many members of our circle of friends have since moved on, some of them several times.

Maintaining friendships is also made more difficult for Anglos by pressures to develop friendships with people of similar incomes and social status. The United States is not a classless society, but rather a society of many social classes, with people frequently moving from one class to another. With each move up the social ladder through advances in employment, education, or marriage, there is pressure to establish new friendships with individuals at that social level in order to solidify one's social position. In Latin America, friendships made in childhood are maintained, while new ones are added. In the United States, friendships are often outgrown, as one advances up the economic and social ladder.

In addition to encouraging people to change residences as well as those with whom they socialize, pressures for economic and social advancement in Anglo culture leave relatively little time or energy for making and keeping friends. U.S. employees work more hours than employees anywhere else in the industrialized world, and their working hours have increased since 1990 (Johnson 2001). Blue laws forbidding commerce on Sundays were lifted in most communities during the second half of the twentieth century, removing restrictions against working on the Sabbath that had been imposed since Biblical times, and making Sunday just another day for economic gain for many businesspeople.

The priority placed on work over leisure and socializing in Anglo culture is also suggested by the relatively few days off given to U.S. employees. Latinos who come to the United States are often startled by the small number of holidays we have off from work, while Anglos living in Latin America are equally surprised by the number of holidays during which work is cancelled.

Anglo visitors to Latin America are also often dismayed by the length of Latino parties. The importance placed on strengthening social ties in Latin America is indicated by the fact that partygoers are typically happy to socialize until late at night, even if they must go to work the next day.

SR:

For several years I helped to train psychotherapists in Monterrey, Mexico, by offering workshops there. Little of such training was being offered at that time in Monterrey, and these workshops were well attended. My hosts would mark the end of each workshop with a dinner party, providing an opportunity to build friendships between myself, the workshop organizers, and the participants. To keep the party going longer, my hosts would not serve dinner until 11:00 p.m., even though the following day was a work day.

I have also presented a number of workshops in the United States. These have invariably ended abruptly at four or five in the afternoon, at which time participants were anxious to return to their own homes.

Join the Club

Faced with so many obstacles to friendship, Anglos frequently join clubs as a means to make and keep friends. They begin doing this in childhood. Preadolescent boys often build makeshift clubhouses to gather in. Only members are permitted to enter, though becoming a member usually requires only that you ask, if the other boys agree. No girls are allowed, though exceptions are sometimes made for girls who show that they are just as brave and tough as the boys.

Though young boys' clubs are usually viewed by adults as only charming or humorous, they serve an important function. Being in a club not only allows them to solidify their friendships and learn about loyalty, but it also gives the boys an opportunity to share their knowledge (even if inaccurate) about taboo subjects such as sex and marital discord, which are almost never discussed in most Anglo homes.

Unlike Anglo boys, preadolescent Anglo girls seldom form clubs with clubhouses and rules. Girls do experience considerable pressure to have "best friends." They often ask each other: "Who is your best friend?" or more plaintively: "Will you be my best friend?" Because one can have only one best friend, most girls are continually experiencing the joy of acceptance and inclusion, as well as the pain of rejection and exclusion, as they are chosen as another's best friend, then later dethroned from this exalted position by another girl. Like other friendships among Anglos, those between young girls tend to be unstable and short-lived.

Joining clubs is also a popular method of seeking friends for high school boys and girls, and even more so for college students. Many U.S. college freshmen join fraternities and sororities in the hope that by doing so they will be surrounded by friends throughout their college years, and that these friendships will be maintained long after they graduate. However, members often lose interest in these organizations by their senior year, and only a minority maintain active friendships with fraternity brothers or sorority sisters after graduation.

Adults in the United States also seek stable friendships by joining clubs. These clubs vary from informal interest groups for people who like to shoot or run marathons or ride Honda Gold Wing motor-cycles, to church-related groups such as the Knights of Columbus for Catholic men or Hadassah for Jewish women, to highly structured and formal organizations such as the Masons.

The Masons, as well as service and social organizations like Civitan, Kiwanis, Elks, and Rotary clubs maintain local chapters in communities all over the United States, as well as abroad, and they recruit members by suggesting that wherever a member goes, the club will provide friendship there. However, when members move from one community to another, they may meet new people through their membership, but the relationships they form are usually superficial ones, and they seldom maintain club friendships from their old community. What these organizations really appear to offer is not organized friendship, but rather organized acquaintanceship.

Anglos and Latinos do not differ in their desire for friendship. Both experience the universal need to be close to others and to share the joys and sorrows of life. However, Latino culture, with its emphasis on interdependence, may place a higher priority on friendship, and the two groups differ in the extent to which their cultures support or present obstacles to making and keeping friends.

Latino culture encourages a stable lifestyle; children in Latin America usually grow up in a single community, often establishing their homes in the same neighborhood as their parents, and they typically keep their friends forever. The *compadrazgo* system adds further stability to friendships by joining individuals and families in a formal relationship which is intended to last a lifetime.

Anglos have no such formal structure to add stability to their friendships. Pressures for economic and social advancement result in a highly mobile society in which most people living in a community at a given time are likely to be from somewhere else, making people often lament, as does the singer-songwriter Carole King: "You're so far away. Doesn't anybody stay in one place anymore?" (1970) Even when they do stay in one place, as people advance up the educational and economic ladder, they often leave their old friends behind, seeking new ones at the same level, in order to stabilize their social positions.

Pressures toward upward mobility leave Anglos little opportunity or time for making and keeping friends. Many join clubs in the hope of finding stable friendships. That stability is likely to remain elusive. More so than Latinos, Anglos find it a struggle to keep friendship in their lives.

 # Morality

MI:

After several years of working as a well-paid research psychologist in Guatemala, I returned to the United States to begin a poorly paid postdoctoral internship in clinical psychology. Though my family faced a period of poverty-level existence, we did own a nearly new Honda Civic, which I had been able to purchase duty-free in Guatemala, because of my United Nations employee diplomatic status.

When I attempted to enter my car into the United States, I was told that it failed to meet U.S. safety standards, and that I could not bring it into this country. With a perfectly straight face, the U.S. Customs agent told me that I had three options: having the car altered (at a cost which I soon learned was nearly equal to its original cost), shipping it back out of the country, or having it destroyed by customs agents. The agent was not unkind, but quite matter-of-fact in explaining the regulations governing this particular situation.

With no money to buy another car, I was forced to ship my Honda back to Guatemala, where I no longer had the diplomatic status to own or sell it. A personal appeal by my wife to the first Guatemalan customs official with whom she met elicited sympathy for our dilemma and appreciation for the absurdity of our "car without a country." He sent her on to his boss, who was equally sympathetic, and even more so when he realized that he had known her father. This kind bureaucrat simply scribbled his name on a piece of paper, granting us permission to sell the car.

Every culture has a concept of morality, or set of principles of right and wrong conduct. These principles vary from one culture to another, and must be learned by each child. What is perfectly appropriate behavior in one culture may be considered immoral in another. The moral principles of each culture, like its particular family structure, reflect the culture's core values, and in turn help to shape the adult behavior of children raised in the culture.

Anything for a Friend

Within Latino culture, morality is more often defined in terms of caring for others and less often defined in terms of abstract concepts of justice than in Anglo culture. Laws are not considered to be the ultimate criteria determining what is right or wrong, and rules are often flexibly interpreted in order to avoid causing suffering.

A good person is considered to be one who is *simpático*. The literal translation of *simpático* is sympathetic. However, the term implies considerably more. A person who is *simpático* is skilled at recognizing social cues and what they indicate about other people's emotional states, and is anxious to assure others' comfort and happiness. Being *simpático* also implies avoiding competitiveness and seeking to reduce conflict, confrontation, and embarrassment.

> **MI:**
>
> *In getting to know Guatemala, I was struck by the unusual degree of tact and social sensitivity in people I met. This seemed less surprising among the educated and sophisticated individuals I dealt with. However, it was also true of many of the humblest Guatemalans.*
>
> *Because of my research, I spent a lot of time in poor, rural villages where farmers and their families were eking out a bare subsistence. These individuals were uneducated and unsophisticated about the world beyond their villages, but they were also simpático, and usually able to put a gauche Anglo stranger who was still learning their language at ease. Many demonstrated manners and social intelligence that put to shame those of the majority of upper-middle-class professionals of my acquaintance in the United States.*

The historical roots of Latino morality lie in chivalry, the code of conduct imposed on knights during the Middle Ages. The tradition of chivalry reached its height during the twelfth and thirteenth centuries in Europe. It required honorable and courteous conduct by the armed and mounted fighting men chosen to be knights, and served as a model of moral behavior for others.

The relationship between chivalry and Latino morality was first clearly described by the Spanish writer Miguel de Cervántes, in his epic novel *Don Quixote*, written in 1604 (2003). Its hero, a middle-aged Spanish gentleman, is so taken with old books about chivalry that he decides to abandon his quiet life in order to become a "knight errant."

He renames and saddles his skinny old stable horse, places a cardboard concoction on his head for a helmet, and embarks on a series of foolish adventures, including attempting to rescue the honor of two "virtuous maidens," who are, in fact, prostitutes. He is assisted in these adventures by his faithful servant, Sancho Panza, who is intensely loyal to Don Quixote, even when Quixote is obviously delusional. Both Don Quixote and Sancho Panza live according to the code of chivalry, by being generous, caring, loyal, and brave, without the expectation of personal gain.

Like Don Quixote, moral Latinos are expected to be respectful and gracious toward women, respectful toward their elders, and kind and helpful to children and to anyone weaker than themselves. They are also expected to be loyal to their friends and family, and courageous in defending those in need of assistance.

Armando, a young and charming *finquero* (rancher) in the fertile lowlands near Guatemala's Pacific coast, demonstrated all of these qualities. A popular companion in the local cantinas, and enthusiastically pursued by a number of attractive señoritas, he still managed to do an excellent job of running his elderly parents' large cattle ranch.

Armando was known for his generosity and for his loyalty to his employees. When one of his workers was overcome by fumes while cleaning a grain silo, he did not hesitate to jump into the silo to save him. He too was overcome by the fumes, and died along with him. In the mourning that followed this tragedy, Armando was often described by grateful members of his community as macho, and a good man, who had done his duty, rather than as an unusual hero.

Shame

Shame plays a major role in maintaining moral behavior in Latino culture. Unlike guilt, which is focused on a person's actions, shame is a more global feeling, focused on oneself. Guilt is more limited, allowing for healing through punishment or by making reparation for the immoral action. Shame is more difficult to remove.

When shamed, a person feels a diminished sense of self, as if his or her lack of worthiness or lovability has been exposed to the world. Metaphors used to describe shame make these feelings clear: "I felt so small I could hide under a penny," or "I just wanted to crawl away." The embarrassment that accompanies shame is often increased by blushing, a physiological reaction that is caused by changes in the vascular system.

When Felipe was a child, his mother would often react to his mischievous behavior by saying to him, "*Que pena*" (How shameful), or "*Me da pena*" (I feel ashamed). She would also remind him "*¿Que pensaría la gente?*" (What would people think?) to drive home the point that his behavior could bring shame not only to himself, but to his entire family.

At times, Felipe's mother also used her community's sensitivity to the powerful discomfort one feels when ashamed to petition for special consideration from others, by saying, "*Me da mucha pena pedir esto, pero…*" (It shames me to ask you for this favor, but …). When she did so, the individual she petitioned in this polite way felt honored to have his power to grant the favor acknowledged, and often bent the rules to accommodate her request.

Feelings of shame will more effectively control behavior in an individual who is a social being, strongly attached to others. Because of the strong sense of connection to others common among Latinos, shame is a particularly effective mechanism for behavioral control in Latino culture.

Sorry, but That's the Rule

Within Anglo culture, there is a longstanding tradition of identifying behavior that is law-abiding as moral, and behavior that is law-breaking as immoral. Laws define what is right or good, and good people obey the law. When laws cause suffering, as they did for the Anglo author when he attempted to bring his car into the United States, it is considered unfortunate but unavoidable.

The emphasis on legalism versus human needs in Anglo culture was evident in the legal dispute several years ago involving the Professional Golfers Association's refusal to allow a tour professional with a rare circulatory disease that made it difficult for him to walk to use a golf cart during tour events (Chambers 1998). It can even be seen in the play of Anglo children, who typically expect much younger children to follow the same rules as older ones when they play a game together.

Insistence on even small children exactly following the rules of games caused difficulty for Michael, an Anglo graduate student in psychology, who was learning the skills of play therapy. A kind and generous individual who enjoyed children, Michael insisted that Tommy, the child he was counseling under supervision at the university's counseling center, follow the rules when they played checkers. His hyperactive and depressed young patient seemed crushed when he lost each of their games badly, but he insisted on playing checkers at all of their sessions.

When Michael's supervisor asked why he didn't change the rules so that Tommy could sometimes win their checker games, Michael was shocked at this suggestion, since he viewed this as teaching the child to "cheat." It was only with considerable coaxing from his supervisor that Michael was able to bend the rules, allowing the child two moves to every one of his own, which resulted in Tommy winning some of their games. By allowing him these small successes, Michael helped his patient to begin feeling better about himself and also helped to cement the therapeutic bond between them.

Michael's difficulty with changing the rules for games played with children during play therapy is not unusual among Anglo graduate students. By contrast, Latino child psychology graduate students, coming from a culture that emphasizes interpersonal needs over abstract principles of justice, typically readily accept the need to rearrange the rules of games for use in play therapy.

The historical roots of Anglo morality lie within Judeo-Christian tradition. They can be traced to the giving of the Law, in the form of the Ten Commandments, by Moses to the Jewish people, as well as to Calvinist Protestantism's emphasis on personal responsibility (Calvin 1989). The association between law and personal responsibility reached its full flower in English jurisprudence, with its ideal of blind justice. According to this ideal, everyone is equally responsible before the law, whether pauper or prince.

While the rule of law is respected in Latino culture, the ideal of blind justice holds less sway, and the practice of asking for, and granting, personal consideration from those in positions of authority is widespread. Even in their prayers, Latino Catholics usually petition the saints, and especially the most powerful of all saints, the Blessed Virgin Mary, to intercede on their behalf with the deity, while Anglos are much more likely to pray directly to God.

Guilt

Within Anglo culture, the desire to avoid feeling guilty plays an important role in maintaining good behavior. Unlike shame, which is focused on the anticipated reactions of others, guilt is a painful individual emotion. Feelings of guilt arise when a person has behaved in a way he or she has been taught was wrong. These feelings focus on a particular action, and they can be removed by undergoing punishment or by making reparation for the action. Guilt is like a debt that can be repaid, but at times the price of repayment can be high.

This was the case for Marian, who had experimented with alcohol and sexual promiscuity in high school. She fought bitterly with her parents over her behavior, until her father died suddenly of a heart attack during her junior year. His death resulted in a period of depression and persistent feelings of guilt that her behavior had caused his death.

An attractive and intelligent woman, Marian punished herself by choosing not to attend college after her high-school graduation, and by allowing herself to become involved only with men who were irresponsible and abusive toward her. She was nearly 30 when a beating by her current boyfriend caused her to be hospitalized, and she decided to enter counseling. Through counseling, she began to see herself accurately, as a talented and worthwhile person, and to overcome her feelings of guilt.

Many Americans have interpreted the differing concepts of morality among Latinos and Anglos as evidence that Anglos possess a higher morality than Latinos. Striking differences do exist between the two cultures in how right and wrong behaviors are defined. These differences do not arise from one or the other culture being more "developed" than the other, but are the inevitable result of each culture's organization and core values.

Befitting a culture that idealizes rugged individualism and fosters comparatively weak family ties, Anglo morality is highly individual. It emphasizes personal responsibility and the rule of law, with feelings of guilt when breaking the law helping to insure moral behavior. Latino morality emphasizes caring for others, loyalty, and respect. Shame, or the feeling that one is not worthy of being loved by others, helps to ensure moral behavior, as befits a culture in which belonging and connection to others is so deeply valued.

Religion

SR:

The first time my Anglo wife Beth visited Colombia with me, she was mystified by the fact that nearly every home she entered, from the most humble dwelling to the most luxurious mansion, displayed a work of art with an identical subject. In a humble home this might be an inexpensive reproduction, while in a luxurious home it was usually an original oil painting. In her experience in the United States, each home had pictures depicting various subjects, reflecting the individual tastes of its owners.

The subject of each of these works of art was Jesus Christ, usually from the waist up, pointing to his chest, with the heart outside his body. The heart was usually illuminated by a candle, and sometimes it was surrounded by a crown of thorns. These works of art represented "El Sagrado Corazón de Jesus" (the Sacred Heart of Jesus).

Beth was unaware that most homes in Colombia display this image because the country is officially dedicated to the Sacred Heart of Jesus. Not only most private homes, but every government office and virtually every place of business in Colombia displays El Sagrado Corazón de Jesus.

There are few ways in which Latino and Anglo culture differ as markedly as that of the role of religion. Latino culture is essentially a Catholic culture, while Anglo culture is characterized by religious diversity. Catholicism is an integral part of Latino identity, while for most Anglos, religious affiliation and cultural identity are distinct. Christians, Jews, Muslims, followers of other religions, as well as atheists all lay equal claim to being Americans, and members of any of these groups would angrily object to the suggestion that their religious beliefs made them less American.

Let a Hundred Flowers Bloom

Religious diversity has characterized the United States since its founding. Among those who colonized North America were Puritans in Massachusetts, Quakers in Pennsylvania, and Catholics in Maryland, all seeking religious freedom. Strong feelings about religious freedom, as well as the religious diversity among the colonists prompted the Founding Fathers to insist on separation of church and state in the U.S. Constitution they drafted.

Most Anglos do believe in God, and most identify themselves as Christians. However, their religious practices have little in common. For example, the churches of Anglo Lutherans and Southern Baptists both assign a central role in their religious beliefs to Jesus Christ, yet their houses of worship could hardly be more different. Lutheran churches are ornately decorated with candles, stained glass, and images of Christ's life and suffering, while Southern Baptist churches are austere, and lack any religious images except an occasional crucifix.

Latino Culture Is Catholic

No such diversity exists in Latin America. Most Latinos are Roman Catholics. Other groups, including Protestants, Jews, and Muslims, are represented among Latinos, and have made important economic, artistic, and scientific contributions to life in Latin America. However, Latino culture is essentially a Roman Catholic culture. The complex and entangled relationship between the Roman Catholic religion and the Latino culture dates back to the 1300s, when Spain was converted to Catholicism, and this relationship was brought to the New World by the Spanish Conquistadors.

Queen Isabella's motives for sponsoring Columbus' voyages of discovery were religious as well as financial. She was as anxious to conquer the *Indes* for Holy Mother Church as she was to obtain their riches for Spain. Isabella believed that the New World would be like Saint Augustine's City of God, where everyone would be Catholic, except the natives, whom she assumed would be easily converted from their pagan religions. It was not by coincidence that Isabella sent Columbus off to discover America in the same year that she expelled all Jews and Muslims who had not converted to Catholicism from Spain.

The zeal of the Spanish for bringing Catholicism to the New World was evident in the names they gave to the cities and towns they founded. Most people assume that the largest city in California is named for angels. In fact, the complete name of Los Angeles is *Nuestra Señora de los Angeles* (Our Lady of the Angels), one of the many names given by Roman Catholics to the Virgin Mary.

Few are aware that the complete name of Santa Fe, the capital city of New Mexico, is *El Santa Fe de San Francisco* (the Holy Faith of Saint Francis). Even most residents do not know that the complete name of Socorro, New Mexico, is *Nuestra Señora de Perpetua Socorro* (Our Lady of Perpetual Help), another name for the Virgin Mary.

Towns founded by the Spanish explorers and Conquistadors read like a catalog of Roman Catholic saints. Within the sparsely populated state of New Mexico, the U.S. state with the strongest Spanish heritage, can be found the towns of San Acacia, Santa Ana, San Antonio, Santa Clara, San Cristóbal, Santo Domingo, San Felipe, San Fidel, San Ignacio, San Jon, San José, San Juan, San Lorenzo, San Patricio, San Rafael, Santa Rosa, Santa Teresa, and San Ysidro, as well as two different San Miguels.

The pervasive influence of Catholicism can be felt throughout Latin America. The Latin American country of Colombia has formally endorsed its relationship with the Roman Catholic Church. Colombia's constitution, unlike the U.S. Constitution, which mandates separation of church and state, not only dedicates the nation to *El Sagrado Corazón de Jesus*, but also stipulates that each president's cabinet must contain a Roman Catholic cardinal.

It is only in Colombia that the government has formally acknowledged its relationship to the Roman Catholic Church. In most Latin American countries, the actions of the government reflect a more subtle blending of culture and Catholicism. For example, Latin American governments have customarily arranged for the construction of "plazas" (main squares) found in most Latin American cities and towns) in front of Roman Catholic churches. It would be inconceivable for a Latin American government to erect a plaza in front of a synagogue or Protestant church, yet the policy of building a town plaza in front of a Roman Catholic church is accepted without question by Latinos.

Mexico attempted to sever its ties with the Roman Catholic Church following the Mexican Revolution because of the Church's close ties with Spain. Until recently, the Catholic Church was barred from training priests in Mexico, and Mexicans who wished to become priests had to obtain their training in Rome, Spain, or the United States. Mexican nuns were also barred from wearing their habits in public until recently.

The influence of the Catholic Church in Mexico has remained powerful, however. Most Mexicans identify themselves as Roman Catholics, and images of *Nuestra Señora de Guadalupe* (Our Lady of Guadalupe), representing the appearance of the Virgin Mary to a poor Indian in 1531 in what is now Mexico City, along with crucifixes, are found everywhere, including in most public school classrooms. The Mexican government has also formally recognized Christmas as a national holiday, and decreed that every employee in the country must be paid each December a Christmas bonus consisting of an extra month's wages (Hernández 2005). Papal visits to Mexico have thrown the country into a frenzy of religious fervor (McGirk 2002).

Even the atheistic Communist government of Cuba has been unable to disassociate itself from the Roman Catholic Church. When Pope John Paul II made the first ever papal visit to Cuba in 1998, its financially strapped Communist government arranged locations for his appearances, provided massive decorations and street cleaning, and even donated public transportation to take the multitude of faithful to see him (Larmer and Nordland 1998).

Throughout Latin America, images of the Virgin Mary, as well as other religious icons, can be found not only in homes, businesses, and classrooms, but also hanging in the front of most public buses. Religious images can even be found in cantinas and houses of prostitution. In rural areas, shrines honoring the Virgin are a common sight on the side of the highway, and the outsides of some buses are elaborately painted with scenes from the life of the Virgin Mary. Even popular Latino songs, such as "*La Guadalupana*," celebrate the Virgin Mary. In Mexico and among Mexicans in the United States, tattoos of images of the Virgin, as Our Lady of Guadalupe are popular, despite the fact that Catholic teachings forbid marking of the body, and images of Our Lady of Guadalupe on T shirts and jackets have become popular icons of Mexican identity.

Latinos who have left the Catholic Church to convert to fundamentalist Protestant churches, which place little emphasis in their theology on the Virgin Mary, often report more distress over abandoning their allegiance to the Virgin than about abandoning the Catholic Church. Many Latino converts simply ignore her lower status in their new churches and continue to keep icons of the Virgin Mary and even celebrate her feast day.

Disobeying the Church

Despite the constant reminders of Catholic faith in Latin America, it would be a mistake to assume that Latino Catholics are in complete agreement with the Catholic Church or that they demonstrate perfect obedience to its commandments. The use of "artificial" methods of birth control (for example, methods of birth control other than the "rhythm method"), which are expressly forbidden by the Church and are considered a mortal sin, are widely used in Latin American communities by Catholics (Bates 2004).

Furthermore, it is virtually the norm for Latin American men to fail to attend masses, as required by the Catholic Church. After adolescence, most Latino men attend Mass only at Christmas and Easter and for family weddings, baptisms, and funerals.

Attendance at Mass among Latin American Catholics is much lower than it is among U.S. Catholics. Unlike Anglos, who usually refer to themselves as ex-Catholics or lapsed Catholics if they have failed to participate in required sacraments for long periods of time, Latinos typically consider themselves Catholics even if they have not attended religious services for years, except for occasional holidays or family weddings, baptisms, and funerals. In this respect, they resemble American Jews, who also typically continue to identify themselves as Jewish despite minimal participation in religious services or rituals.

In the United States, being a Catholic has always involved revering both the teachings of the Church and its priests. Recent revelations of sexual abuse by priests both shocked and saddened the faithful. By contrast, in Latin America there exists a robust tradition of anticlericalism. Many Latinos are devout Catholics, while at the same time rejecting the priestly establishment.

SR:

My abuela, *who considered herself a staunch Roman Catholic, was famous for her violent anticlericalism, refusing to have anything to do with priests. Since the time of* La Conquista *(the conquest), the Catholic Church in Colombia has allied itself with the most conservative political forces. The Church supported the Spanish monarchy against the liberation movement in Colombia and later supported the Conservative party. My* abuela *was a Liberal who loved the Church, but hated its priests.*

When my grandmother was on her deathbed, our well-meaning parish priest attempted to enter and administer the last rites of the Roman Catholic Church. Dying was apparently not sufficient reason for Abuela to miss getting in a last gibe at the unfortunate priest, and she demanded that that vampiro *(vampire) be thrown out of her house.*

My Religion Is No Laughing Matter

Even Latinos who are anticlerical Catholics, as well as those who fail to attend Mass or otherwise choose to ignore the directives of the Church, usually feel a deep sense of loyalty to their Catholic faith. Most Anglos consider their religious affiliation to be just one of many aspects of who they are, like their occupation, city of residence, age, marital status, and so on. For Latinos, being Catholic is a more central and emotional element of their identity.

Because of the strong emotional connection that most Latinos feel toward Catholicism, they may take criticisms of the Catholic Church as a personal affront, and jokes about the Church are likely to be viewed as insensitive or offensive. Just as with issues of race and color, Catholic jokes are best told by Latinos themselves (and they often are).

Though the majority of Latinos in Latin America and the United States continue to identify themselves as Catholics, Protestant and Mormon missionaries have had some success in converting numbers of people in Latin America. However, because of the close association between their cultural identity and the Roman Catholic religion, attempts to convert Latinos away from Catholicism, like marriage of a child to someone outside the Church, are likely to be experienced as an assault upon their culture and their families, rather than just upon their religion.

Missionaries in Latin America have often had more success in converting entire families than single individuals. In the United States, when one member of a family converts to a different religion, his or her family may feel disapproval or disappointment, but (with the possible exception of Jewish families) they generally do not view conversion as an insult to their family. Because Catholicism is such an integral part of Latino culture and family life, a Latino who converts independently of his or her family is likely to face intense family disapproval and pressure to reconsider this decision.

SR:

One of my patients, a young man from a middle-class Catholic family in Monterrey, Mexico, suffered not only disapproval, but effective banishment from his family that drove him to emigrate to the United States when he joined the Jehovah's Witness Church. He had become interested in the church after talking to missionaries who visited Monterrey. When he mentioned this interest to his parents, his father told him in no uncertain terms that he should not leave the Catholic Church, and his banishment resulted from the decision to convert to another religion. Years afterward, this young man and his family are still estranged.

Successful missionaries take into account the importance of the Latino family. One such individual who has developed a following among Latinos in the Southwestern United States is the radio evangelist *Hermano* Bernal (Brother Bernal). *Hermano* Bernal promotes "family nights" and instructs his listeners to ask God's help for all of their family members rather than seeking personal salvation. One of his most popular promotions has been a miraculous "family cloth" doused with holy oil, which listeners are advised to rub on each member of the family.

The constant presence of Catholicism in Latino culture is unexpected for most Anglos, who are accustomed to confining their spiritual involvement to Sunday mornings, in their secular society. Even Jewish Latinos can be heard to mutter "*Jesús, María, y José*" (Jesus, Mary, and Joseph) when upset. However, like non-Catholic Latinos, most Anglos who come to Latin America are soon accustomed to the fact that Catholicism is woven into the fabric of Latino life.

CHAPTER NINE

Thinking Styles

SR:

When I was six or seven years old, my mother told me a story she had been told by her mother. The story concerned a boy who had raised his hand to his own mother. Somehow, I knew before she described the horrible consequences of his act what these would be: his arm froze in the air and remained frozen there. My mother described how neither physicians nor the family's parish priest could return the offending arm to its normal position.

Naturally, the boy learned his lesson from what had happened to him, and from that day on, he was a good and dutiful son. With his arm upraised in the air he became an excellent student, though he was handicapped in the sports and games his classmates played. He grew up to be successful and respected in his community, a good husband, and a loving father. To all who knew him, his upraised arm was a reminder both of his sin and of his redemption.

When the man died, it was impossible to close his coffin because of his offending arm, and it was necessary to bury him with the coffin open. In Antioquia, my province of Colombia, it is the custom to disinter the dead after three years and to move their decomposed remains to a small box. When this man's remains were disinterred, it was found that he had turned to dust, except for his arm, which was intact and still upraised.

Now my mother is an old woman, and I must care for her like her parent. I have spent the last thirty-five years of my life as a scientist, teaching and doing research at a university. As a scientist, my armor is logic and skepticism. I know that my mother's story cannot be true, but how can it not be?

MI:

I was first introduced to the "scientific method" in the fourth grade at Boulevard Elementary School. In language appropriate to our ages, my classmates and I were taught that scientists followed a systematic procedure that included careful observation, assigning objects to different classes, forming hypotheses about these classes, and testing hypotheses through experiments that employed rigorous logic. We were assured then and in each subsequent science class that this scientific method was a powerful tool for understanding the world around us.

It was not difficult for our teachers to convince us that scientific thinking was the most effective kind of thinking. While I was in school, U.S. and Russian scientists were putting rockets and then human beings into space, and medical researchers like Dr. Jonas Salk were conquering deadly diseases. It seemed like there was nothing science could not achieve, given the will to do so. My friends and I dreamed of growing up to be white-coated rocket scientists or physicians, rather than poets or clergymen.

Thinking is what most distinguishes human beings from other species, and it is an activity in which we are almost always engaged. Even when we sleep, our thinking continues, in the form of dreaming. Across cultures, there may be few if any differences in thinking ability, but there are important differences from one culture to another in thinking styles.

Logic or Intuition?

Latinos and Anglos begin life with the same basic mental equipment, but they are taught by their families and encouraged by their cultures to think in very different ways. Anglos idealize thinking that is straightforward and logical. They believe that the universe is based on logic, and that it will yield up its secrets to logic and experimentation.

Anglo stories reflect this belief. They follow a logical sequence and have a beginning, a middle, and an end. As they proceed, they reveal the who, what, where, when, and why of events. The novels of the American writer Mark Twain follow this pattern. In *Huckleberry Finn* (2005) for example, the journey of Huck and Jim, the escaped slave he befriends, down the Mississippi River is described from its beginning to its inevitable end. Though a fictional tale, it proceeds without ever defying logic, and is therefore easily understood and believable to the reader.

Most Latinos have less faith in logic. They know the world is mysterious, contradictory, and frequently illogical. They believe that human understanding is most likely to come through the more passive processes of contemplation, intuition, and acceptance of contradiction.

The more intuitive approach to thinking of many Latinos is even seen in the working style of their psychotherapists. Manual therapy, a logical, step-by-step approach to alleviating such psychological problems as depression, anxiety, and obsessive-compulsive disorder, has become popular among U.S. therapists. Many therapists prefer this approach because it eliminates doubts about how to proceed with a patient, and its effectiveness has been demonstrated in clinical studies. Pressures on therapists from managed care health insurance companies who pay for psychotherapy to document and justify everything they do with their patients and to help them in the shortest time possible have also led to the widespread adoption of manual therapies.

Psychotherapists in Latin America have, by and large, rebelled against such a rigid approach to psychotherapy, insisting that they cannot possibly know what to do at any given moment with each client. Such decisions cannot come from a manual for these therapists, but only from their clinical intuition, which is gained through years of training and experience.

Latino literature also reflects this hesitancy to rely exclusively on logic. Latino stories, like children's fairy tales, are often meant to enchant, rather than to explain. The greatest Latino writers are surrealists like Gabriel Garcia Márquez, the Colombian author of *One Hundred Years of Solitude* (1970). In that epic multigenerational novel, one young man is murdered on the town plaza after Sunday Mass. His blood forms a river which flows down the street to the house of his mother, climbs the stairs to her door, enters the house, flows up a wall to avoid ruining her precious carpet, then crosses her kitchen to stop at her feet. She looks down and says, "My son is dead."

Go Do the Right Thing

While striving to be logical, Anglo thinking attempts to eliminate emotion from the decision-making process, identifying feelings as antithetical to logic. To many Anglos, it does not seem strange when the popular personal advice guru Dr. Laura Schlessinger urges her listeners to ignore their feelings and "go do the right thing" (Schlessinger 1996).

Most Latinos see no such need to separate reason and emotion. Any personal advice guru who would tell a Latino audience to ignore their feelings when making a decision would find few sympathetic listeners. If logic without emotion is the Anglo ideal, reasoning that includes feelings is the Latino ideal. "Doing the right thing" for Latinos means considering your own and others' feelings in all deliberations. The prototypical Latino hero is Cervántes' Don Quixote, who is revered because he follows his heart even when it leads him to do things that contradict logic and common sense.

The Latino belief that the mind and the heart should be joined is also demonstrated in more subtle ways. The prestigious Universidad Téchnologica in Monterrey, Mexico, unlike U.S. schools of science and technology, is almost equally renowned for its symphony hall and its programs in music and the visual arts. This is roughly the equivalent of M.I.T. and Julliard sharing a campus.

"Can Do" or "No Way"?

In addition to being logical and free of emotion, ideal Anglo thinking is goal oriented. Every problem is assumed to have a solution and can be solved if one tries hard enough. The first hero of generations of Anglo children is *The Little Engine That Could* (Piper 1995), a hardworking little train that is mocked by bigger trains until faced with the insurmountable task of climbing a gigantic mountain. Undaunted, the Little Engine struggles forward with the determination that characterizes Anglo heroes of literature and films, chanting, "I think I can, I think I can, I think I can." The Little Engine finally succeeds, then chugs joyfully down the other side of the conquered mountain chanting, "I thought I could, I thought I could, I thought I could."

Optimistic, goal-oriented thinking has produced impressive successes. It has made possible the settling of the frontier, the conquest of many diseases, and the landing of astronauts on the moon. It has also contributed to less clearly beneficial outcomes such as the development of nuclear weapons.

Latino thinking often contrasts with Anglo can-do thinking. Latino culture encourages a more passive response to the world. Faced with a difficult or impossible situation, the typical Latino response is likely to be a rueful smile, a shrug, and the statement "*Ni modo.*" "*Ni modo*" means, literally, "No way," and implies that there is a limit to our resources and our ability, but no limit to the frustrations and disasters to which human beings are subject.

The difference between the "can do" approach to the world favored by Anglo culture and the *ni modo* approach more often encountered in Latino culture can be seen in the way individuals and their families react to a diagnosis of the most malignant forms of cancer, which have a low survival rate. With such a diagnosis, most Anglos will aggressively pursue every possible medical avenue, no matter how painful, costly, or uncertain the outcome, until no more options are available. When the battle against cancer is subsequently lost, the Anglo victim's family is likely to be comforted by the knowledge that they did everything they could to try to save their loved one. Many Anglo families will even continue the battle after the victim's death by contributing, or asking their friends to contribute, to cancer research.

A Latino patient with the same grim diagnosis and the same resources often has an easier time recognizing that if he or she travels far from home for medical treatment, the ordeal is likely to be not only expensive and painful, but also unsuccessful, and that it may be better to stay at home and make the most of the time remaining. After the family member's death, the Latino family is more likely to be comforted by knowing that they did everything they could to make their loved one as comfortable as possible at the end.

A Tingling on the Back of His Tongue

As is true of many other aspects of Anglo and Latino culture, characteristic thinking styles of the two are mirror images of one another, each approach with both its strengths as well as its limitations. The straightforward, logical style of thinking favored in Anglo culture is effective in identifying problems and evaluating potential solutions. However, much of the heavy lifting in creative thought and scientific discovery comes between these two activities, and does not proceed in a straightforward, logical manner.

Once a problem is identified, thought frequently goes underground, in what psychologists have described as an "incubation phase." There, hopefully, it proceeds through mysterious unconscious processes which appear to involve more intuition and embracing of contradictions favored by Latino culture than the straightforward logic favored by Anglo culture. The solution to the problem is first felt, rather than known, and then finally emerges whole like a butterfly from its cocoon. Albert Einstein once wrote that solutions to the immensely complex problems of physics he struggled with signaled their arrival to him as a tingling on the back of his tongue, before emerging to his consciousness (1952).

The power of intuition was demonstrated at a U.S. psychoanalytic institute where candidates for analyst positions were traditionally interviewed by each analyst on staff, who would then meet together and review their impressions of the candidate. They would then summarize their reasons for accepting or rejecting him or her. One candidate made an excellent impression on every member of the staff except one, who could give his colleagues no logical reasons why he felt that this individual had serious emotional problems which would be likely to interfere with his ability to function as an analyst.

The candidate was accepted at the institute, based upon the highly favorable impression he had made on almost everyone. However, within a month of his arrival, he proved to be a chronic complainer and inept in his work. Shortly afterward, he suffered a nervous breakdown.

The institute staff met to discuss what had happened, and urged the one analyst who had rejected the candidate, even predicting his breakdown, to reveal how he had known so much about this individual. With some embarrassment, the analyst (who was very short) admitted that his assessment had been based on illogical intuition; he had a "feeling" about the way a person treats short people being a key to their psychological stability, though he could not logically explain why this should be the case. Among Latinos, he would not have felt obligated to do so, since intuitions are considered respectable data.

Logical and Positive Can Be Negative

The favored Anglo approach to decision-making, which attempts to eliminate emotion from the process, has its value, as well as its limitations. It is often advisable to put aside personal feelings and preferences in order to make choices which are hard, but fair to everyone affected by the decision. For example, U.S. society's legal mandate that job candidates be chosen on the basis of merit rather than on the basis of their race, religion, or gender requires that personal feelings or arbitrary preferences not enter into these selection decisions.

Yet, the Latino approach to decision-making, which emphasizes the importance of considering personal feelings, also has its place. It is not wise (or perhaps even possible) to make important personal decisions with only your head and not your heart. Attempts to choose a husband, a career, or even a house or car through only cold logic are likely to result in choices which do not bring happiness.

Bruce, a young U.S. Air Force officer, attempted to use logic to decide whether or not to marry his longtime girlfriend. He drew a line down the middle of a sheet of paper and painstakingly listed the advantages of marrying her on one side and the disadvantages of doing so on the other. Since the list of advantages turned out to be longer than the list of disadvantages, Bruce asked her to marry him, and she accepted. His inability to know whether he wanted to get married without resorting to such a simplistic exercise in logic should have been a warning to Bruce that he was not ready for marriage; he lacked the maturity to make the compromises necessary for a successful marriage, and the couple soon divorced.

Too much emotion in decision making can also create problems. An excessively emotional decision about when to tell a man she was dating that she loved him almost ruined the promising relationship of Carla, a Latino beauty queen. Born in Puerto Rico, Carla won the right to represent her adopted state in the upcoming Miss America pageant. Though strikingly beautiful as well as outwardly poised, she struggled with anxiety and insecurity, and had never had a boyfriend.

Through psychotherapy, Carla overcame her anxiety enough to begin a romantic relationship. However, she shocked her boyfriend by deciding to declare her love for him for the first time at a supremely inappropriate moment. She did so at the holiest time of year for Catholics: on Good Friday during the Exposition of the Blessed Sacrament, while both were on their knees in double genuflection (the only time of the year when Catholics kneel on both knees). Fortunately, the young man got over his shock, and eventually the couple married.

Like the insistence on separating logic and emotion, the "can do" problem-solving approach to the world idealized by Anglo culture also has advantages as well as drawbacks. Though the optimistic belief that every problem has a solution and that everyone can succeed if she tries hard enough has helped to make the United States a wealthy and powerful country, it is often unrealistic. Unfortunately, every problem does not have a solution. Our most deeply desired goals are sometimes unrealizable, our treasured relationships eventually end, and death inevitably defeats us.

One Anglo couple experienced the tragedy of the death by hanging of their fifteen-year-old son. Not only were they overcome with grief at losing a child they deeply loved, but they suffered equally by blaming themselves for not preventing his death. Both the boy's father (who had frequently instructed his children "Never say you can't") and his mother tormented themselves ceaselessly about what they should have done to save him.

In fact, they were exemplary parents who had done everything possible to help their son when he became depressed: they obtained therapy for him, arranged for him to be prescribed antidepressant medication, and entered family therapy. Furthermore, they had always been caring and available to their children, and when their son entered adolescence they had nicely balanced his need for supervision with his need for privacy. Though they had been remarkably good and compassionate parents, they remained convinced that they had failed their son. The father stated, "I'll go to my grave convinced that there was something I could have done."

Anglos are taught to believe that there are no limits to what they can achieve. Yet many in U.S. society do not succeed even by the most modest standards, and some find themselves out of work and unable to feed their families because of economic upheavals over which they have no control. Programmed only for success, Anglos who experience anything less than success often feel as if they were failures. Every time the U.S. unemployment rate rises, so does the number of suicides in this country (Lester 2000).

The Upside of Looking Down

Like the Anglo "can-do" attitude, the Latino attitude of "*ni modo*" also has its place and its limitations. A "*ni modo*" approach to the world can result in passivity and submission when "can do" might make it possible to find a way to overcome obstacles.

A member of the Franciscan religious order in Monterrey, Mexico, for many years held as his greatest spiritual ambition to go to the United States and work with Native Americans. He felt deeply saddened about the treatment of Native Americans by members of his religious order who had accompanied the Spanish explorers to the American West, and he felt that he had a special calling to assist their descendents.

However, he spoke little English and could not realize his ambition without mastering this language. Learning English as an adult is difficult for a native speaker of Spanish (more so than learning Spanish is for an adult English speaker), but doing so is not impossible. When it was pointed out to him that he made it virtually impossible for himself to master English by spending nearly all of his free time in the company of Spanish-speaking friends rather than seeking out English speakers with whom to practice their language, his response was, "*Ni modo, estos son mis amigos*" (What do you expect me to do–those are my friends). His response to his dilemma was to passively avoid making the considerable effort and sacrifice necessary to achieve his dream.

However, the Latino *ni modo* is often more than passive submission. By accepting that there are limits to our power to control the world, and no limit to the ways the world can cause us to suffer, Latinos have been able to survive oppression and natural disasters with their dignity and their faith intact. Latin American societies have experienced crushing blows during the past century, only to arise after each and begin rebuilding.

MI:

I was amazed at the resilience of Guatemalans after the devastating earthquake of 1976. With an absence of self-pity, they endured the hardships of losing their homes, their possessions, and for some even their loved ones, and immediately began putting their lives back together. This was even more remarkable because it came during an already difficult time of economic hardship and political violence for the country. After this experience, it came as no surprise to me to meet Guatemalans in the United States who had made great sacrifices to get here, and were uncomplainingly working 16 or 18 hours a day at two or three menial jobs in order to provide a better life for their children than they had had.

The difference between the Latino acceptance of fate and the Anglo belief in the inevitability of success is nowhere more evident than in the way each culture deals with death. Latinos have an abundance of rituals and ceremonies surrounding death, and even celebrate a holiday, *El Dia de los Muertos* (the Day of the Dead), which acknowledges death's power over us and grudgingly accords death a place of honor. Most Anglos observe few death rituals and prefer simpler funerals, during which they allow themselves to express less emotion that that typically seen at Latino funerals. Anglos also tend to be more reluctant than Latinos to talk about death; they have invented a number of euphemisms, such as "passing away."

This reticence led to a recent misunderstanding following the tragic death on the operating table of a New Mexico teenager struck by a drunk driver. When the surgeon who had tried to save his life reluctantly told the boy's mother that he was "no longer breathing," she replied, "Well, at least he's not dead."

The more logical, unemotional, and goal-oriented thinking style favored by Anglo culture and the more intuitive, emotional, and accepting thinking style favored by Latino culture are each well suited to some circumstances and poorly suited to others. Creative thinking and discovery begin with logic, but proceed with contemplation and intuition. Some decisions require that personal feelings be ignored, while others require that they be considered. A "can do," goal-oriented attitude can result in high levels of achievement, but can also result in despair when a problem proves to be insurmountable, while a "*ni modo*" attitude can result in passive submission, but can also bring about acceptance and survival. Neither the style of thinking favored by Anglo culture nor that favored by Latino culture alone is sufficient to meet all of life's challenges.

PART III

Latinos in America

In the preceding chapters, we have examined the differences between Latino and Anglo families and childrearing techniques, as well as the distinct values and behaviors that result from these differences. Many of our examples have come from Latin America, the source, via Spain, of Latino culture.

In the remaining chapters, we focus specifically on Latinos now living in the United States, describing what may be distinctive about the expectations and behavior that Latinos bring to the American workplace, school, marketplace, and voting booth. Latinos living in the United States vary in the degree to which they have become acculturated to U.S. mainstream culture, and an additional chapter examines Latino acculturation. A final chapter looks at cross-cultural romantic relationships between Anglos and Latinos.

Latinos in the Workplace

SR:

Several years ago, I grew tired of paying rent and purchased a small office building with a colleague for my psychology practice. We didn't have the time to maintain the grounds surrounding the building and were fortunate to find Leonel, a Mexican immigrant who was employed by Wal-Mart, but needed extra jobs to support his large family, to work for us.

By chance I learned that Leonel's family was devoted to San Martín (Saint Martin), a dark-skinned saint popular with working-class Latinos. Like many Latino families, they had devoted a corner of one room in their home to the saint, but they owned no images of San Martín except a small, poorly reproduced picture. On one of my trips to Mexico I came across a statue of San Martín, and decided to purchase it as a gift for my employee.

Leonel was conscientious and dependable, and he was popular with his bosses at Wal-Mart, who eventually promoted him to a supervisory position. As be began earning more money, I heard that Leonel had given up his other side jobs, and worried that we would lose him. I asked him if he was going to stop working for us, now that he was earning a better salary. He answered "Nunca obvidaré el doctor de San Martín (I'll work for the "San Martín doctor" for as long as you need me).

Like most immigrants to the United States, the majority of Latinos who come to the U.S. do so in order to find work that will provide a better life for them and their families. Latino workers bring with them varying skills, as well as attitudes and expectations that differ from those of most Anglo employees. Understanding these differences can help to make their working relationships more successful for both the Anglo employer and the Latino employee.

I'm Not My Job

Among the differences between typical Latino and Anglo workers is that of how each views the meaning or significance of work. There is a moral imperative to work in Anglo culture that is based on the Calvinist association between idleness and immorality (Calvin 1989). Furthermore, since most Anglo families are not comparatively closely knit and ethnic identity has been blurred by generations of intermarriage, many Anglos define their identity not through their family background, but through their work.

The same is not true of most Latinos. Work is generally viewed in a more utilitarian way in Latino culture; it is a means to get the things you and your family need or want. Personal identity comes primarily from your family membership. Whereas in Anglo culture where you get to largely defines your identity, in Latino culture your identity is primarily defined by where you came from.

The strong Anglo association between work and morality does not necessarily hold in Latino culture. In the poorest strata of Latino societies everyone, regardless of gender or age, must work. When a family in Latin America has achieved a higher income level, it is considered a requirement only that the father must work. Mother or older children may work, but it is not an expectation that they do, and it is considered a proud achievement if a man makes enough money that his wife and children do not have to work. It is almost unheard of in a traditional Latino family, but common in Anglo families, for a mother and teenaged children to be employed when the father is a wealthy professional or entrepreneur making two or three hundred thousand dollars or more a year.

Getting Along with the Boss

Differences in how children are socialized in Latino and Anglo families also result in differences in how Latino and Anglo employees relate to their bosses, as well as to their coworkers and even to an organization itself. Latino employees tend to relate to their bosses as they would to their own parents, accepting authoritarian behavior more readily than Anglo employees, and they are less likely to question a boss's decisions and directives.

In addition, *personalismo,* or the personal relationship between employees and their supervisors, is usually viewed as less important by the Anglo employee than by the Latino employee. Anglos are generally accustomed to following a clear set of guidelines or rules governing their behavior at work and in their interactions with their supervisors, with these expectations clearly spelled out in employee handbooks.

Employee handbooks are not unknown in Latin American companies, but Latino organizations tend to be less bureaucratic and to rely less on handbooks in judging employees. While not unimportant to most Anglo employees, pleasing the boss and avoiding getting on his or her bad side is a more crucial issue for most Latinos, for whom success on the job and obtaining raises and promotions is likely to be dependent upon their ability to please their bosses in their home countries. Seeking to establish a close relationship with them, it is not unusual for Latino employees to invite their supervisors to their homes or to family events such as baptisms or *quinceañeras.*

Latino employees also expect their bosses to treat them with courtesy and respect, to be aware of their personal contributions to the organization, and to take an interest in their lives outside of the workplace. When such behavior is not forthcoming from their bosses, Latinos employees are more likely than their Anglo counterparts to interpret this as meaning that their efforts for the company are not valued, or that they are doing a poor job.

Demonstrating to the Latino employee that his or her efforts are valued is not difficult. Even simple gestures such as learning the names of employees' spouses and children are appreciated, and sending home gifts for the employee's family communicates that the employee is a valued member of the organization. For Latino employees who have left their homes in Latin America in order to better their families' standard of living and suffer the conflict of having to be far away from their families while working hard to support them, flexibility in permitting visits home for holidays and important family events creates loyalty and assures the retention of valuable Latino employees.

The Latina employee is as appreciative of such gestures from her bosses as her male counterpart. In addition, for her the issue of respect may be of even greater importance. Raised with the expectation that she will be treated with special deference and respect because of her gender, the Latina employee is likely to resent attempts at too much familiarity by male supervisors or the use of any vulgarity in her presence. Because this is less true of female Anglo employees, successful supervision of Latinas may require greater sensitivity by Anglo male bosses than some are used to demonstrating.

Coworkers or Friends?

While the distinction between home and workplace is often indistinct in Latin America, a strict distinction between the two is generally maintained in the U.S. workplace. Anglo etiquette requires that you discretely avoid intruding on the privacy of your coworkers, and particularly in larger organizations it is possible for an Anglo employee to not know the names of the spouse and children of a coworker with whom they have worked closely for years. Anglo workers are also less likely than Latinos to discuss family crises with coworkers.

Latino workers usually make it a point to learn about their coworkers' families, and they generally know the names of coworkers' spouses as well as their children. While Anglo etiquette requires not intruding, Latino etiquette requires that you inquire about the well-being of coworkers' families. Involvement with coworkers also extends beyond the workplace. Latinos are more likely to invite coworkers to family events, including baptisms, children's birthday parties, Holy Communion and confirmation parties, and weddings.

This custom surprised a professor who had recently been hired by the University of New Mexico Psychology Department, when he was invited by a native New Mexican Latino colleague to the Holy Communion party of his daughter. He did not know his Latino colleague's children, and would never have been invited to such a family event in his native Michigan. He was even more surprised when he arrived to find that the party was a huge event attended not only by relatives, but also by a large number of university colleagues, as well as other family friends.

This degree of involvement with coworkers has positive as well as negative consequences. A positive consequence is that the atmosphere in the workplace is less bureaucratic and more relaxed and personal than that of most U.S. workplaces. However, the more family-like the workplace, the greater the possibility of the same types of jealousy and hurt feelings that can occur in family life.

For Anglo employees, being turned down by the boss for a requested schedule change would probably produce only disappointment. However, for Latino employees, who are accustomed to a family-like atmosphere at work, this experience may produce feelings of personal rejection.

A Little Respect, Please

The Latino employee is more likely than the Anglo employee to view gender as an important determinant of behavior at work, and to feel more uncomfortable carrying out duties associated with the opposite sex in Latin America.

> *SR:*
>
> *My brother owned a popular restaurant in Colombia for many years. On one occasion, the woman whose job it was to sweep the sidewalk in front of the restaurant before it opened for business missed work because of illness. My brother told the short order cook, who earned the same amount as the woman who swept, to sweep the sidewalk before beginning his food preparations.*

The cook responded that he wanted to help, but that he could not sweep because that was a woman's job. When my brother told him that he might lose his job if he refused to sweep, the cook pleaded that he needed his job, but that he couldn't possibly sweep because "no era digno" (he would lose his dignity).

Exasperated, my brother grabbed the broom and swept the sidewalk himself, then asked the cook: "¿Perdí algo de mi dignidad?" (Do you see any of my dignity missing?) The cook answered: "No, porque tú eres el jefe" (No, because you're the boss), indicating that being the boss allowed him, but not a lowly worker, to redefine social conventions.

Latinos as well as Latinas also expect that women will be treated with greater deference and respect because of their gender. If two Anglo workers approach a water fountain, the first to arrive, whether a man or a woman, is likely to drink first. In a Latin American workplace and for Latinos employed in the United States, it would be considered boorish and rude for a man to drink from a water fountain before first allowing the woman, who may have arrived after him, to drink. Such behavior may be seen as quaint or old-fashioned in Anglo culture, but it is considered simple good manners by Latinos.

Work groups in the United States often develop a level of good-natured bantering which includes at least some mild vulgarity. It is often considered a mark of acceptance for a female coworker to be included in these bull sessions, and a matter of pride for her to be able to banter as crudely as "the boys."

MI:

During the 1970s the all-male University of New Mexico Psychology Department was struggling to become more diverse. Two female faculty members were hired in quick succession, but both had difficulty fitting into the department, and each left within a year of being hired. The third was different. A child development specialist who later published a popular book on gender, she managed to nicely balance career, marriage, and motherhood.

Her coworkers quickly learned that Ruth, unlike her female prede-
cessors, was unshockable, and she clearly enjoyed being "one of the boys."
She won over her male colleagues by hanging out with them, and by
often knowing the best off-color jokes of anyone in the department.

By contrast, in the Latin American workplace male colleagues, as well as
supervisors, are expected to be circumspect around female coworkers,
carefully avoiding the use of any vulgarity, and the same expectation is
usually brought to their U.S. workplace by Latino employees. Latinas
are careful to give a wide berth to bantering sessions that threaten to
violate the rules of polite conversation. To do otherwise would compromise the respect they receive as women.

Because gender is such a significant issue in Latino culture, the
Latina boss or business owner expects to be treated with a double dose
of respect and deference—first as *jefe* (actually, "*jefa*," to indicate gender), and second as a woman. Latina bosses are generally highly
capable people who have demonstrated their strength and individualism by defying the Latino cultural norm of males being in charge.
Their early social training also created the expectation that they
would be treated with respect due to them as women, which becomes
compounded with the respect due to them as bosses.

Are Latinos More Loyal?

Socialization in close-knit families also affects how Latino employees
view their connection to the organizations that employ them. Latinos
are raised to place the good of their families above personal advancement, and this collective orientation is usually extended to other organizations with which they become affiliated.

As Chong and Baez (2005) point out in their excellent book on
Latinos in the workplace, *Latino Culture*, Latino employees very often
demonstrate a degree of loyalty to their employer unusual among
Anglo employees, valuing a long-term relationship with their company
above the salary increase or step up the career ladder that may come
with moving to a new employer. As Chong and Baez note, the Latino

employee typically feels committed to return in hard work what they have received in trust and support from their employer, and they may view Anglo job hopping as a result of character flaws or excessive, unhealthy ambition.

Latinos and Anglos differ in both their views of work and their expectations about how they and their employers should behave. Because of their dedication and loyalty, Latinos often make exceptional employees, and making cultural accommodations for them, including sensitivity to their needs for *personalismo* and respect, are well worth the effort.

CHAPTER
ELEVEN

Latino Students

SR:

My education in U.S. schools, and that of my three older brothers, began disastrously. Though we were told repeatedly by our parents that we must respect our teachers and behave well in school, it was hard for us to do so. We understood little English, and we were frightened and confused. I tried to disappear into the woodwork and not be noticed. My big brothers reacted differently. They let everyone know that they wouldn't be pushed around and were soon singled out as troublemakers.

All of our difficulties came to a head when an Anglo student pushed me out of line at the drinking fountain. My biggest, toughest brother, Al, defended the Roll family honor by rewarding the offender with a bloody nose. The principal quickly resolved our adjustment problem by expelling all four Roll boys from his school.

Our parents next enrolled us in a parochial school. Fortunately, our teachers there were more understanding, and there were no more expulsions. When we did get into trouble, our parents invariably sided with our teachers.

On one occasion, some of my classmates and I sneaked out of Daily Mass to buy treats at a bakery with our lunch money. When we tried to sneak back into the school, we found Sister Gabriel standing at the gate with her arms folded over her ample bosom, glaring at us. My Anglo friend whispered to me that if she hit him, he was going to tell his dad. Already well aware that I was going to get punished again when I got home, I thought that was the stupidest thing I'd ever heard.

Among human relationships, that between teachers and their students has the potential to be one of the most mutually satisfying; most teachers want to teach, and most students want to learn. The majority of adults can recall at least one teacher who changed their lives, and many teachers report feeling profound satisfaction in having touched the lives of their students. However, when a teacher and her students are from different cultures, as is now often the case for Latino students in U.S. schools, the relationship can be frustrating for both teacher and students.

Obstacles

Educating Latino students represents both a considerable challenge as well as an opportunity for the U.S. educational system. Minority children, most of whom are Latino, have already become the majority in schools in two states, California and New Mexico, and because of high Latino birth rates this will likely happen also in several other states.

Latino parents tend to place great faith in education as a way for their children to achieve a better life, as well as a way to become a better person. The term *educada* is used by Latinos to describe a person who has completed many years of formal education, as well as someone who is well-mannered, respectful, kind, and tactful toward others. No such association is assumed in Anglo culture. One study of Latino parents' attitudes about education found that nine out of ten Latino parents expected their children to attend college (Schmidt 2003). However, despite the hopes of their parents, Latinos have the highest school dropout rate of any ethnic group in the United States (Garcia and Sanchez 2007). According to the Pew Hispanic Center, in 2005 only 62 percent of all Latino adults in the U.S. had completed high school, as compared to 93.6 percent of Anglos. Other studies have found that high school completion rates for African Americans fall between these two figures, and those for Asian Americans are comparable to those for Anglos (Garcia and Sanchez 2007).

The problem of high dropout rates is even more acute for Latino children born abroad. The President's Advisory Commission on

Educational Excellence for Hispanic Americans (1999), found a high school completion rate for foreign born Latinos of only 40 percent.

Disparities in the educational attainment of Latinos and Anglos continue at the college level. In 2002, the percentage of Anglos over the age of 25 who had earned a bachelor's degree (29.4 percent) was nearly three times that for Latinos over the age of 25 (11.1 percent).

Latino children in U.S. schools, particularly those born abroad, struggle with learning a new language and a new culture. Furthermore, many of their parents are fleeing poverty and have themselves had only limited opportunity for formal education in their home countries. In many of these children's homes there may be few if any books or other reading materials even in Spanish.

In addition, illegal immigrant Latino children may lack the motivation to succeed in school because of their immigration status, and, many Latino children eventually decide that it is a waste of time for them to graduate or go to college, because they lack the documentation needed to obtain legal employment (Zuckerbrod 2007).

Problems such as immigration status and lack of parental education cannot be solved by the schools. Nevertheless, despite formidable obstacles, teachers can help Latino students to be more successful in the classroom. To achieve this, they must be aware of the differing cultural expectations and learning styles that the Latino student brings to school.

Who's the Boss?

Many of the differences between Latino and Anglo students result from differences in family structure and childrearing practices. One such difference is the way teachers are viewed. As an authority figure as well as an individual who is *educada*, a teacher, the Spanish translation for which is "maestra" or "maestro" (literally, master), occupies a position of considerably higher status in Latino culture than in Anglo culture.

In the Latin American classroom, the teacher's word is law. Latino children are expected to never question the pronouncements of their teachers, just as they are not expected to question the decisions of their parents. They are expected to show deference and respect toward all of their teachers, and particularly toward their female teachers, who merit respect both because of their position of authority, as well as their gender.

Ironically, the high status of teachers in Latino culture has created its own problem for Latino immigrants to the United States. Among Latino students who are successful in school and go on to obtain college degrees, a disproportionate number choose to enter teaching, because of its high status in the culture, as well as the opportunity it offers to contribute to the lives of others. Fewer Latinos choose science and engineering careers, though these fields pay well and they also offer the opportunity to contribute, in a less personal way, to the community (Mack and Jackson 1993).

Because of their expectation that teachers will function as powerful authority figures, Latino students are often confused by Anglo teachers who try to play the role of a buddy and to lessen the distance between themselves and their students. If teachers do not clearly establish their authority and no one appears to be in charge in the classroom, Latino students may be more likely than Anglo students to get into trouble. This risk is often increased by the frustration they experience because of language difficulties, resulting academic problems, and the belief that their minority status marks them for prejudice.

The Power of *Personalismo* (The Personal Touch)

Because of their culture's emphasis on *personalismo*, Latino students are likely to be more sensitive to the quality of their personal relationships with their teachers than Anglo students. It is a truism among educators that students tend to perform better when they are taught by teachers who take an interest in their lives, but the teacher's *personalismo* may be an even more crucial determinant of motivation to succeed in school for the typical Latino student than for the typical Anglo student, whose culture stresses individual achievement more strongly.

Because of the closeness of Latino families, it is also of particular importance that the teachers' *personalismo* extend to the Latino student's family as well. Personal contact with Latino parents increases the likelihood of student success by emphasizing the teacher's regard for the student, as well as her or his authority. In addition, establishing a personal relationship with their parents reduces the risk that the Latino student will come to view the English-speaking, Anglo-designed school and Spanish-speaking Latino home as alien to each other, and reject one or the other as irrelevant.

Regular contact with the parents of Latino students can also help to avoid misunderstandings and potential conflicts. Though Latino parents are disposed to be very supportive of their children's teachers, if a Latino parent believes that a teacher is mistreating their child, cooperation can turn to defensiveness and a stance of opposition. Within the shame-oriented Latino culture, parents will go to great lengths to avoid being shamed or having their children shamed. If a Latino parent concludes that a teacher has shamed their child by holding him or her up to public ridicule, the teacher can lose an important ally. Teachers of Latino children would therefore be advised to confront student misbehavior privately, as well as to respectfully share with parents their concerns regarding a student's behavior.

Different Is Good

In addition to bringing different expectations about teaching to the classroom than their Anglo classmates, Latino students may also approach learning differently. While Anglo culture idealizes cognition that is logical and goal oriented, Latino culture encourages thinking that is more intuitive and contemplative. As a result, the typical Latino student may learn in a more passive way, and be more comfortable than most Anglo students in receiving, rather than discovering, knowledge.

Consistent with this learning style, which is seldom favored in U.S. schools, it is traditional in Latin American schools for the *maestra* or *maestro* to tell the students what they are supposed to learn, and there is a greater emphasis on rote memorization. While this orientation may discourage divergent thinking by Latino students, it may also give them an advantage in situations where memorization is required, such as in learning the multiplication tables, state capitals, French verbs, or the hundreds of bones in the human body.

Despite the emphasis on rote learning in Latin American schools, the culture's encouragement of intuition and contemplation helps to produce individuals with high potential for creativity in the arts and sciences. This is true because the most crucial phase of the creative process does not involve logic, which is emphasized in Anglo culture, but rather the ability to think intuitively, which is emphasized in Latino culture.

Latino culture also encourages the integration of thinking and feelings, while Anglo culture favors "objective" reasoning, divorced from emotion. Latino children typically grow up more comfortable expressing emotion and making it a part of their reasoning and decision making. The ability to do this may make them better prepared than most Anglo children to master subjects that involve human emotions, such as music, art, literature, and even the social sciences.

Comfort with their emotional life may also encourage a more widespread appreciation of the arts in Latino culture than in Anglo culture. Within Anglo culture, there tends to be more interest in the arts among individuals with greater formal education. In Latin America, this is less true.

Although a college education is not a necessary requirement for appreciating the arts, relatively few Anglos who have not had the benefit of a higher education have heard of the influential American painters Jackson Pollock or Mark Rothko, and Nobel laureate William Faulkner, who created an imaginary county that captured the essence of the American South, is read in this country mostly by well-educated individuals. By contrast, it is difficult to find anyone in Mexico who is unfamiliar with the Mexican painters Frida Kahlo or Diego Rivera, and Nobel laureate Gabriel Garcia Márquez, who created an imaginary province that captured the soul of Colombia, is widely read throughout Latin America by waiters and taxi drivers, as well as by doctors, lawyers, and teachers.

Despite the unique strengths that their cultural background provides them, many Latino children struggle in U.S. schools. The

challenge facing their teachers is to unleash these students' considerable potential for learning and creativity. To achieve this, they must
help their Latino students overcome the language barriers and cultural
differences that have produced such high dropout rates in the past. If
they are able to teach authoritatively, demonstrate a genuine interest in
the lives of their students, and establish a working alliance with parents,
they are much more likely to be successful.

CHAPTER TWELVE

Latino Customers

SR:

I often shop at a produce market in Albuquerque, New Mexico, which was always full of Latino families whenever I arrived. The management made it a practice for a number of years to give a washed apple, plum, or other seasonal fruit to each child as their parents left the store. When a new owner purchased the business, he immediately discontinued this practice as a way to reduce his expenses. Anglo customers continued to arrive in equal numbers, but the number of Latino customers dwindled to a fraction of what it had been previously.

I suspected the reason why this had happened, and my suspicion was confirmed when I had the opportunity to ask some of the market's former Latino patrons why they no longer shopped there. They stopped shopping there because this small gift given to their children had been accepted by the parents as a token of respect and appreciation for their loyalty. It was important to them because it signified that their relationship with the former proprietor was not merely economic. They had no reason to feel this way about the new owner.

Every society has marketplaces where buyers and sellers can meet and exchange money for goods and services. In an African village, the marketplace may consist of a small cleared piece of land where sellers gather to spread out their wares on the ground for sellers to examine, while in a city in Europe or the United States, it can be an indoor shopping mall consisting of dozens or even hundreds of stores, covering many acres.

The process of buying and selling that takes place in these large or small marketplaces seems as if it would be a straightforward one. However, as is true of every other social activity, the details of shopping are shaped by culture, and Latino shopping patterns differ from those of Anglos.

Latino population growth in the United States is expected to continue to be robust for the next several decades (Garcia 2003). As their numbers grow, so will Latino disposable income, which has already been estimated at nearly a trillion dollars a year (Chong and Baez 2005), and it is not surprising that U.S. businesses are eager to attract Latino customers.

Like Anglo shoppers, Latinos look for high quality and low prices when purchasing goods and services. However, just as Latino workers bring different attitudes and expectations than Anglo workers to the workplace, Latino customers bring different attitudes and expectations to the marketplace.

Keeping Up with the Garcias

For example, Latinos tend to associate their purchases, and the stores they frequent, with social class. Anglo shoppers may be more willing than Latino shoppers to shop in whatever store offers the lowest prices. Much of Wal-Mart's success in the United States has been due not only to its discount pricing, but also to the fact that it offers a broad range of products at a range of prices, and is therefore able to attract customers across a wide economic spectrum. Upper-class Anglos may joke about shopping at Wal-Mart, but they continue to shop there to obtain the most competitive prices.

Most Latinos in the United States are working class, struggle economically, and are happy to shop at Wal-Mart or other discount stores. However, upper-middle-class and upper-class Latinos prefer to avoid stores whose primary clientele is working class or lower. Within Latin

America, members of these classes may speak with pride of having never entered a discount store, or of having visited one only out of curiosity.

In every U.S. city with a large Latino population, increasing numbers of Latinos are starting to enter the ranks of professionals and of middle and upper management. As they do so, they provide customers anxious to demonstrate their economic and social achievement through their purchases. Retailers can take advantage of this desire by providing specialty stores that allow Latinos to distinguish themselves from the working-class Latinos who shop at Wal-Mart and to demonstrate their entry into the upper and middle classes.

Although discount stores full of working-class Latinos do not attract more well-to-do Latinos, stores that offer luxury items at discounted prices do. Outlet malls near the Mexican border, like the one in San Marcos, Texas, with stores such as Polo, Guess, Coach, and Liz Claiborne, are usually full of upper-middle and upper-class Mexican families who have driven from Mexico to do some serious shopping.

It is not only well-to-do Latinos who purchase prestige brand merchandise. Even for economically hard-pressed Latinos, prestige brands often have greater significance than they do for most Anglos. When a Latino has managed to emerge from poverty sufficiently to have some discretionary income, a flashy pair of Nikes is not simply an expensive purchase but also a mark of achievement and a statement to the world that he or she is no longer poor. A retailer who wishes to attract Latino business should address both the fact that most Latino families struggle to live within their means and also the fact that most will also purchase luxury items whenever possible.

Recreational Shopping

Latino shoppers differ from Anglo shoppers in other ways as well. Latinos are more likely to shop in larger groups consisting of several family members. Latinos tend to view their shopping trips as a family outing or social event. Unlike Anglos who run into acquaintances in a store, Latinos will almost always stop (because it is considered rude not to do so) and take the time to introduce everyone in their group to those they meet and to exchange news and gossip about people they know in common.

Like other social events, a shopping trip for Latinos is also often accompanied by eating, and a store that wishes to attract Latino shoppers would be wise to have some food items available for purchase. Even the availability of candy is likely to attract more Latino shoppers and to keep them in the store longer.

The Latino commitment to family offers additional opportunities for retailers. Mothers who are shopping for themselves are likely to feel better about their shopping trip if they are able to make at least a small purchase for their children. Accommodating this may dictate unconventional store arrangements. For example, locating the toy section next to women's clothing allows Latino children to be entertained while their mother is able to concentrate on her shopping, as well as allowing her to conveniently purchase a treat for her children.

The Latino commitment to family also dictates that store displays and merchandise selection accommodate that commitment. Latinos may purchase gifts and cards for birthdays, Mother's Day, and other holidays for more individuals than Anglos, including extended family members, godparents, and godchildren, and reminders to do so are likely to be effective.

The Power of *Personalismo*, Again

Doing business in Latino culture has traditionally involved more than an impersonal exchange between buyer and seller of money for goods or services. It has also, whenever possible, included a social dimension or *personalismo*. Latinos tend to establish a personal relationship with those with whom they do business.

At times, the boundary between business relationships and friendship can become indistinct for Latinos, as it did for Flora, a Mexican immigrant living with her family in the town of Socorro, New Mexico. When Flora decided to supplement her family's income by making and selling tamales by the dozen, her small business quickly flourished. Her tamales became popular treats both among the many Mexican families who were native to the area, as well as among local Anglo families.

Many of Flora's customers also became her friends. She and her customers exchanged Christmas gifts, they invited her to their homes, and when Flora's oldest daughter graduated with honors from the local high school, a number of families who had been her clients attended the party she and her husband gave to celebrate the event.

The hectic pace of Anglo culture, as well as the size of many retail organizations, makes it considerably more difficult for sellers to establish a personal relationship with buyers than it was for Flora. Nevertheless, it is possible to introduce elements of *personalismo* into business practices, and this is likely to attract more Latino clientele. In addition to their cultural preference for *personalismo*, many Latinos in the United States feel unwelcome and alienated, and gestures reminding them that their patronage is welcomed are noticed and appreciated.

One of the most obvious gestures is advertising in Spanish. A number of retail businesses have started advertising in Spanish, including Wal-Mart, which has had a national TV advertising campaign urging Latino shoppers to come in *para tu familia* (for your family's sake). Store displays in Spanish as well as English are also appreciated, while hiring Spanish-speaking employees not only makes an obvious statement that a business welcomes Latino clients, but also attracts Latinos who feel more confident speaking Spanish.

Practicing *personalismo* successfully requires that employees are selected and trained to treat each customer as a valued individual, rather than as an anonymous consumer. Large business organizations can incorporate *personalismo* into their operations by placing a higher priority on ensuring that their staff is personable, courteous, and responsive.

However, smaller businesses have a considerable advantage in practicing *personalismo*. They can endear themselves to Latino shoppers by recognizing and acknowledging repeat customers as *buenos clientes* (good customers), by greeting them by name and by commenting on the attractiveness and good behavior of their children.

Showing courtesy and *personalismo* toward Latino shoppers is particularly important not only because it creates customer loyalty but also because it generates effective word-of-mouth advertising. Because of their culture's emphasis on interdependence, Latinos tend to have broader social networks than Anglos, and to share more information with friends, acquaintances, and relatives.

When a Latino shopper finds bargain prices or has been treated with *personalismo* by a business establishment, she or he is likely to tell many others about it. When they feel they have been treated discourteously, the negative repercussions of their experience are also likely to be widespread, and a single act of employee insensitivity can drive away many potential customers.

Every city or town in the United States with a significant Latino population seems to have one or more thriving *mercados* (markets) or *carnicerias* (butcher shops). These are usually popular with local Latinos, even though their prices may be higher than those of larger nearby chain stores.

One reason these stores do so well is that they stock some items popular in Latin America that cannot be found elsewhere. However, much of their success in siphoning business away from Anglo stores is the result of their *personalismo*; Latinos like shopping in neighborhood *mercados* or *carnicerias* because they are among the relatively few establishments in the United States that do not treat business as a mechanical exchange of money for goods and services.

By adding a dimension of respect and friendliness to their business transactions, Latino proprietors are able to attract and retain many Latino customers. Anglo business owners, by practicing *personalismo*, can also attract a number of loyal Latino customers. An added benefit is that they are likely to attract more Anglo customers as well.

Latinos in the Voting Booth

MI:

In the midst of the 2008 presidential primary campaign, an old friend, a lawyer who has been very much involved in the political life of his country, told me: "If I were a Norteamericano, I'd vote for Hillary Clinton for president. This surprised me, both because my friend has been affiliated with a conservative political party, and because I knew him to be quite traditional in his views, including those having to do with gender roles. I asked him why he would vote for her, and he responded that he admired Hillary Clinton for her strength and intelligence, and that he had been impressed by the dignidad (class) she had shown during her husband's Monica Lewinsky scandal. Other Guatemalan friends later expressed similar sentiments to me about Ms. Clinton.

That Latinos and Anglos may approach politics differently does not come as a surprise to many U.S. citizens, having witnessed from the relative tranquility of their own country the turbulence which has characterized political life in much of Latin America. The reasons for that turbulence are historical and complex, and beyond the scope of this book.

Like Anglos, Latinos want leadership that will provide them with safety and prosperity. However, cultural differences between the two groups often lead Latinos to employ different criteria than Anglos in choosing their leaders.

A Sleeping Giant

The potential importance of Latino votes has been a subject of interest since the national elections of 1960, when some writers described the Latino vote as a "sleeping giant" (García 2003). By the time of the 2000 elections, Latino voters constituted 8 percent of the U.S. electorate, were being described as the "soccer moms of 2000" (García 2003), and were actively courted by both Republican and Democratic candidates for national and local office.

However, contrary to expectations, the Latino vote did not make a critical difference in the extremely close presidential race of 2000 (Garcia and Sanchez 2007). It also did not make a difference in the presidential election of 2004. In that election, the largest states, California, Texas, and New York, each produced lopsided majorities among Latino voters for the candidate who would have carried the state without them (Garcia and Sanchez 2007).

Latinos held 3,251 elected positions in California in 2007 (Hispanic PR wire), and a Latino, Antonio Villaraigosa, has served as mayor of Los Angeles. However, voter registration has not increased over several years among the large Latino populations of New York state and Arizona, and Latino political power in those and other states has not grown as expected (García 2003).

Across the U.S., Latinos eligible to vote in the 2000 and 2004 presidential elections exercised their right to do so in significantly lower numbers than Anglos. In 2000, only 57 percent of eligible Latino citizens registered to vote versus 72 percent of Anglos. In 2004, these figures were 58 percent vs. 75 percent (Garcia and Sanchez 2007).

Among the explanations students of U.S. politics have offered for these differences in voting rates has been that many Latinos have felt alienated from and powerless to affect U.S. politics (Garcia and Sanchez 2007), and that Latinos are cynical about the democratic process, coming from countries where that process is so often subverted through election fraud, voter intimidation, or a choice of candidates whom potential voters believe are corrupt. Central and South American voter participation, with the exception of Colombia, where all eligible citizens are required to vote, is the lowest of any region in the world (Highton and Burris 2002).

Low voter participation among Latinos is also believed to be influenced by the fact that many self-identify according to their country of origin, as Mexicans, Colombians, Puerto Ricans, and so on, as opposed to "Latinos" (Garcia and Sanchez 2007). Because they do not see themselves as members of a huge and potentially powerful group of voters, this may give Latinos less incentive to vote.

Despite obstacles, the sleeping giant of Latino political power is awakening. A surge in Latino political awareness and involvement occurred in California following passage of Proposition 187 in 1996, which limited immigrants' access to social services and education (it was subsequently declared unconstitutional by the courts), and of Proposition 227, in 1998, which ended bilingual education programs. The passage of these propositions was widely perceived by Latinos, including those of the second or third generation in this country, as motivated by racism (García 2003, Garcia and Sanchez 2007).

The current immigration debate appears to be creating the same heightened political awareness and interest in voting among Latinos (Constable 2007). As political awareness among Latinos increases, a pan-Latino identity (García 2003, Garcia and Sanchez 2007, Porter 2001) is growing, nurtured by the popularity of Spanish language TV networks such as Univision, which serve as a kind of pan-Latino media town hall, and by intermarriage between Latinos from different countries of origin.

A potentially even greater factor in the growth of Latino political power is the high birth rate among Latinos, which has been estimated to be six times the overall U.S. birth rate (García 2003). The children of Latino immigrants who are born in this country are automatically U.S. citizens, regardless of whether their parents are here legally or illegally. They, along with their parents who are able to obtain citizenship, will inevitably swell the already sizable ranks of eligible Latino voters.

Family Values

Latino voters in the United States, with the notable exception of Cuban-Americans, have traditionally been strong supporters of the Democratic Party (García 2003, Garcia and Sanchez 2007). Most Cuban-Americans, strongly focused on their opposition to Fidel Castro, have allied themselves with the Republican Party, which they have perceived as more hostile and unbending toward Castro's Cuba.

In the 2000 and 2004 national elections, George W. Bush and the Republican Party were able to effectively portray themselves as the guardians of family values. By doing this and by extensively targeting the Latino electorate with Spanish language TV ads and appearances in heavily Latino-populated locations, Bush was able to win 40 percent of the Latino vote in 2004, up from the 21 percent received by Bob Dole in his 1996 Republican presidential bid (García and Sanchez 2007).

Despite Bush's effective use of the family values banner, it is the Democratic Party that has mostly been perceived by Latino voters as the party that cares about families, demonstrating this with their greater support for social welfare programs, health care reform, education, and a living wage. The perception that the Democratic Party supports families, as well as the perception that many Republican lawmakers are anti-immigrant, based on their positions during Congressional debate over immigration reform, helps to explain why Latino support of the Democratic Party continues to grow (Bowler, Nicholson, and Segura 2006). A hot-button issue for Latinos has been the separation of families through deportation of illegal immigrant parents from their children born in the United States, something viewed with particular horror by Latinos, but not apparently by Anglo hardliners who insist on the need to deport illegal immigrants. By enforcing the law regardless of human cost, these individuals emphasize the difference between traditional Anglo and Latino conceptions of moral behavior.

For many Latinos, recent cases of families separated through a parent's deportation carry unpleasant echoes of the Elían Gonzáles case. During the battle over whether or not the six-year-old Elían should be reunited with his only surviving parent in Cuba, most Republican lawmakers demanded that he remain in the United States. Among Latinos, only Cuban-Americans typically agreed that separation from his father was justified, in order to prevent Elían from having to live under Fidel Castro (Garcia and Sanchez 2007).

Charisma

In addition to their preference for candidates who are seen to strengthen families, Latino voters may also prefer charismatic leaders who are able to strongly inspire identification with them, and loyalty. The same is no doubt true of Anglo voters as well, though being able to inspire voters may be less crucial to political success in the United States.

Among those who have been elected to the highest office in the United States are some who have famously lacked charisma. The most taciturn and unapproachable of these men was probably "Silent Cal" Coolidge. Coolidge was vice president under Warren G. Harding. He ascended to the presidency upon Harding's death in 1923, and was re-elected in 1924 despite the fact that he was said to be "shy, retiring, and somber" (Gilbert 2007, 1032). Coolidge was once approached at a state dinner by a woman who told him that she had made a bet that she could get him to say more than two words. His reply was: "You lose" (1032). When the witty writer Dorothy Parker was told that Coolidge had died, she asked: "How can they tell?" (Sherrin 2005, 86).

The power of identification with leaders and of loyalty in Latin American politics can be seen in the adulation Eva Peron generated in Argentina, as well as the personal popularity Fidel Castro enjoyed in Cuba despite the nearly 50 years of deprivation that Cuban citizens have suffered under his rule (Canadian Broadcasting Company 2006, British Broadcasting Company 2007).

The U.S. presidents of the last 50 years arguably most admired in Latin America are John F. Kennedy and Bill Clinton. Kennedy's considerable popularity in Latin America was increased by his initiatives in the region, including the Alliance for Progress, an ambitious attempt to reduce poverty and social inequity (Lowenthal 1991). Clinton generated great affection despite the United States' unpopular interventions during the decade preceding his presidency. Once when speaking before the National Assembly of El Salvador, Clinton even received a standing ovation from members of the leftist FMLN party who had belonged to guerrilla groups suppressed with the help of U.S. arms and military advisors (Engler 2007).

Among the qualities that inspire identification and loyalty among Latinos is *personalismo*, or the ability of their leaders to speak to them in a way that communicates genuine interest and caring about their personal welfare. John F. Kennedy had this talent, and moved millions when he told a German audience "*Ich bin ein Berliner*" (I am a Berliner) and when he requested Americans to "Ask not what your country can do for you; ask what you can do for your country." Bill Clinton also had this gift, as did Ronald Reagan and Franklin Delano Roosevelt before him.

Politics and Marital Fidelity

Anglo and Latino voters also differ with regard to the importance they place upon marital fidelity in their leaders. Most Latinos are less upset than Anglos by male infidelity (but not female infidelity). The alleged infidelity of John F. Kennedy (Hersh 1997) and the Monica Lewinsky affair, over which Bill Clinton was nearly impeached, have done little to lessen the affection of Latinos for either.

What is of great importance to most Latinos is a man's respect for his family, and his discretion. John F. Kennedy and Bill Clinton were both seen as good fathers and family men, and each remained in their marriages. They were largely forgiven by Latinos for their infidelity. Latino voters are likely to be less generous toward other politicians, such as 2008 Republican presidential candidate Rudy Guliani, who is not only known to have to been unfaithful to his wives, but has broken up his family by divorcing twice.

Madam President

While this book was being written, U. S. voters were considering the candidacy of the first female contender for president of the United

States. Many Anglos believe that Latino men are macho and chauvinistic and Latino women powerless and dependent, although the truth is more complicated. It is in Latin America that four women have served as presidents of their countries, Lidia Gueler Tejada of Bolivia (1979–1980), Violetta Chamorro of Nicaragua (1990–1996), Michelle Bechelet of Chile (2006–), and Cristina Kirchner of Argentina (2007–). A fifth woman, the enormously popular Eva Peron of Argentina, would likely have also been elected had she not died of cancer at the age of 33 in 1952. Latino culture, at least since the reign of Queen Isabella of Spain in the fifteenth century, has welcomed powerful women leaders.

Latinos who are raised in healthy families grow up appreciating maternal power. The Latino wife is expected to use subtlety in wielding her power, outwardly deferring to her husband and indulging her children. However, Latino children know they must not displease or ever disrespect their mothers, and Latino husbands are equally aware that if they wish their lives to remain pleasant and tranquil the decisions they make for their families must be ones that do not displease their wives.

Latina executives in Latin America as well as Latinas who are teachers are often more powerful and respected than their male counterparts because they are able to demand the respect due them as women, as well as that due them because of their positions of authority. Latinas in positions of authority are expected to show respect for the female role, demonstrating this through their devotion to their families, their attention to their appearance, and their decorum. As long as they do so, they may in fact enjoy more power and respect than most women are able to obtain in Anglo culture.

Latino voters do not have difficulty voting for a woman for president, as long as she possesses the qualities of strength and *personalismo* they admire, and she demonstrates respect for the female role. Many Latinos supported Hillary Clinton during her 2008 presidential bid, feeling that she demonstrated that respect by staying in her marriage despite her husband's infidelity, by raising, with her husband, an impressive daughter, and by focusing on issues involving the needs of children (Clinton 1996) and health care.

Advice to Candidates

To gain their support, candidates for public office must convince Latino voters that they will work to support families. Following the rash of recent tawdry scandals involving politicians who were elected under the banner of "family values," both Anglos and Latinos are understandably cynical about the issue of family values. However, Latino voters will continue to support candidates who demonstrate a commitment to the real family values of providing a better life for children, the elderly, and the poor.

Under the specter of terrorism, both Anglo and Latino voters want a president who will provide for the security of the United States. Voters are likely to use different yardsticks to measure each candidate's ability to provide that security, including his or her military policy and foreign policy experience. Latino voters are also likely to choose a leader whose *personalismo* and charisma inspire their trust and communicate to them the strength needed to face threats to our country.

Gender may be a less important variable for the Latino voter than for the Anglo voter. Latinos will vote for either a male or female candidate who exhibits qualities of charisma and *personalismo*. In addition, a male candidate must be viewed as a man of strength who has respect for his family, and a female candidate as a woman of strength who has respect for her femininity.

CHAPTER FOURTEEN

Latino Acculturation

SR:

When I moved with my family from Medellìn, Colombia, to the United States, many things were confusing for me. I was disgusted by the strange food that people ate here, and in the absence of our familiar diet I was now obliged to eat it as well. I found Anglo behavior also mysterious and disturbing, and people seemed cold and unfriendly compared to Colombians.

My greatest difficulties occurred at school. My parents have told me that I was a talkative and precocious child, and I was quite able to defend myself among my older brothers, and to assert myself at home. I took a big step backward when my parents enrolled my brothers and me in school.

All of the boys in my class had a crush on the pretty and vivacious young nun who was our teacher, and I was no exception. At recess, rather than playing ball, they would surround her on the playground, vying for her attention by talking about their exploits, and she invariably listened with rapt attention. I yearned to do the same, but felt terrible frustration that because of my limited English, I could not.

Because of my poor English, I struggled even more in class. I couldn't understand our classwork, or what we were expected to do for homework. The only exception was spelling. I had grasped that we were expected to learn to spell four new words each night, and that we would be tested on those words the following day.

I was determined to do this assignment perfectly because I knew I could, and I did not misspell a single word all year. My kind teacher, who understood my difficulties, made me feel smart and successful for that small triumph. As my English improved, I became a better student. Unfortunately, I was apparently born a terrible speller, and I have never been able to repeat that early spelling success.

Latinos living in the United States vary in their degree of acculturation to U.S. mainstream culture. Newer arrivals are usually the least acculturated, though this is not always the case, and it is helpful when meeting a Latino for the first time to know how to judge his or her degree of acculturation, something we will explain in this chapter.

Learning How to Be an American

Anglos and Latinos learn their own cultures as children. With little or no conscious awareness, we learn how to act, think, and believe from our families, our teachers, and our classmates, as well as from television, movies, and even the Internet. Learning another culture, or acculturation, is a more conscious and deliberate process than learning one's own culture.

The task of learning how to function in a new culture can be daunting because there are an infinite number of details that comprise a culture's expectations. These details range from what time to get up in the morning and go to bed at night, to what foods are appropriate to eat, how to go about making friends, express romantic interest in someone, or address your boss or teacher. Each culture has its own unique answers to questions such as these.

Immigration 101

One of the concerns frequently expressed about the influx of Latino immigrants into the United States is that they will not become integrated into the mainstream culture. The fear that U.S. culture could be overrun by hordes of alien immigrants is not a new concern. A dire warning that the influx of new immigrants so different from the rest of us that they would never assimilate like past immigrants, and therefore posed a grave threat to the culture was issued not recently by opponents of legalizing the status of Latino immigrants in this country, but by Benjamin Franklin, in 1751, about the arrival of German immigrants into colonial Pennsylvania (Tichenor 2007).

In 1854, the Know Nothings, a nativist political party, successfully influenced the U.S. Congress to increase restrictions on immigration by fanning fears that Irish immigration would result in American society being controlled by the Pope (Condon 2007). In 1911, the Dillingham Commission established by the U.S. Congress published a 41-volume report warning that immigration from Southern and Eastern Europe was in danger of subverting American society. Their warnings helped to obtain passage in Congress of the immigration quota acts of the 1920s (Zeidel 2004).

Fears that immigration will degrade U.S. culture are based on the assumption that a nation's culture is fixed and eternal, yet also fragile and needing protection. In reality it is none of these things. Anglo culture is constantly evolving, while at the same time robustly maintaining core values that continue to serve the society well. Contrary to the fears of Benjamin Franklin (who later mellowed in his views about German immigration), the Know Nothings, and the Dillingham Commission, Anglo culture did not become Germanized, Italianized, or Armenianized, and the United States did not come under the control of the Pope.

Anglo culture has absorbed aspects of the cultures of each wave of immigrants; those who had arrived earlier adopted the newcomers' customs that they found most appealing. While this culture borrowing was going on, each immigrant group over time was becoming more assimilated to U.S. mainstream culture.

The same is true of Latinos. Mexican-Americans whose families had resided in what is now the U.S. Southwest since long before the 1848 treaty of Guadalupe-Hidalgo ended the Mexican-American War and extended citizenship to the Mexicans living in the region, nearly all speak perfect English, participate successfully in all aspects of American life, and frequently intermarry with Anglos. Early Puerto

Rican immigrants after U.S. citizenship was extended to residents of the island in 1917, and Cubans from the earliest wave of immigrants following Castro's takeover in 1959 are also mostly well assimilated.

Because of their strong family tradition, many in these groups have also retained their Latino core cultural values regarding the importance of family, religion, and *simpatía*, while becoming well integrated into the U.S. mainstream. The same pattern is likely to continue for more recent Latino arrivals in this country.

MI:

Two friends of mine, both Native New Mexican Latinos, met in high school in their small town in northwestern New Mexico. The families of both Anita and Chris had lived in New Mexico for generations, and their parents had grown up on small farms in a rural area of the state where life resembled that described by Rudolfo Anaya in his popular novel Bless Me Ultima *(1999).*

Attending their town's public schools, both of my friends had been forbidden by school authorities to speak Spanish at school, even on the playground, and though they had learned Spanish before English, as adults their Spanish was not fluent. Spanish continued to be the primary language of their parents. Their mothers, who had not been employed outside their homes, spoke English haltingly all their lives.

Both Anita and Chris were good students, and both gravitated naturally toward helping professions. Anita stayed at home, studying nursing at the local community college, while Chris studied social work at the New Mexico State University. After completing their educations, they married and elected to live in a larger town only a few minutes away from where they had grown up, in order to be close to their families.

My friends wanted a large family, but unfortunately were only able to have one child, an outgoing girl whom they named Maria after the grandmother who had died a few years before her birth. A good student and as charming as her mother, Maria was very popular with her classmates, and she was elected president of her class during her senior year in high school. Since she had been a little girl, she had wanted to become a pediatrician, and after high school graduation she enrolled as a pre-med student at the University of New Mexico.

As adults, Anita and Chris continued to attend Mass at the same Catholic Church they had attended as children, and they were active in the local Right to Life organization. Despite this, they approved of their daughter's Anglo, non-Catholic fiancé, when she fell in love during her senior year at the University of New Mexico.

Maria brought her new boyfriend home to meet her parents shortly after she began dating him, and her parents found him to be a well-mannered and hard working young man from a nice family. They also knew that he supported their daughter's goal of attending medical school, as well as her intention to eventually practice medicine in her home town. They also did not object to their daughter getting married in her fiancé's church, which she elected to join in order that their children would have as strong a religious foundation as she had had.

Still Latino?

Rather than being homogeneous, Latinos in the United States demonstrate many degrees of acculturation to the dominant Anglo culture ranging from having little knowledge of the rules of behavior and the social skills needed for success in this society to being so adept at acting like Anglos that those who meet them express amazement when they learn that they are from "somewhere else." Among the most acculturated Latinos are some individuals, particularly Mexican-Americans, who were born in the U.S. whose families have been in the U.S., or what is now part of the U.S., for generations.

Showing appropriate cultural sensitivity requires determining to what extent the Latinos with whom you are dealing are acculturated to Anglo culture. The less acculturated a person is, the more crucial it becomes to modify your behavior in dealing with that individual. For Latinos who are highly acculturated to Anglo culture, this is much less important. Under certain circumstances, your behavior could be perceived as offensive.

The most reliable clue to determining an individual's degree of acculturation is language. The extent to which a Latino has mastered English functions as a rough guide as to how much they know about Anglo culture. This is true because the difficult process of learning a language almost always indicates interest in the people who speak the language, and usually requires considerable contact with native speakers.

Other important clues about a person's degree of acculturation are provided by the extent to which he or she makes their cultural background obvious. Such clues include how a person chooses to dress, how they address others, and their topics of conversation. For example, Latino adolescents who dress very much like Anglo adolescents and Latino adults who dress like middle-class Anglos are usually relatively well acculturated.

Similarly, the form of address used in talking to others is another indicator of degree of acculturation. Less acculturated Latinos generally retain the practice of addressing people with whom they are not well acquainted in a very polite, formal way, unlike Anglos and highly acculturated Latinos, who usually address others less formally. Unlike English, which employs the same verb forms for addressing everyone, Spanish verbs indicate whether you are addressing a person with whom you are not well acquainted (*Usted* form), or someone with whom you have a close relationship (*tú* or *vos* forms).

An individual's topics of conversation also offer clues about his or her degree of acculturation. Less acculturated Latinos often make frequent reference to their cultural background. If you were to meet two Cubans who have been in the United States for the same amount of time, it is likely that for the less acculturated of the two, his or her Cuban heritage would be a prominent topic of conversation. The more acculturated Latino may never even bring it up.

Latinos Who Reject Their Culture

Among Latinos in the United States are a few individuals who are disdainful of their culture, and do not wish to be identified as Latinos. Such individuals are particularly likely to be found in communities such as those along the U.S.-Mexican border, where negative stereotypes of Latinos are prevalent.

Identifying with the economically and politically dominant culture and rejecting one's own cultural heritage is not confined to Latinos.

During the Second World War, some Jewish inmates of the Nazi concentration camps attempted to dress and act like their brutal Nazi guards and to adopt their hateful stereotypes of Jews (Bettleheim 1980). In the United States, the writer James Baldwin noted that some African Americans, including his own mother, responded to his dark skin as if it were dirt (Baldwin 1995).

SR:

One of my patients in Albuquerque, New Mexico, where Latino culture is not disdained, but in fact is highly regarded, demonstrated this rejection of his own Mexican heritage. When he graduated from college, he insisted on having the Italian version of his name placed on his diploma, rather than the name given to him by his parents.

Though the first language Pablo had learned was Spanish, he refused to speak it, and when addressed in Spanish would refuse to answer. Though Albuquerque is home to dozens of excellent Mexican restaurants, he insisted on taking business associates to one of the few local Italian restaurants, where he insisted on ordering in Italian, much to the confusion of his waiters, almost none of whom spoke a word of Italian.

When Pablo decided to seek psychotherapy, he mistakenly chose me as his therapist, not realizing that I was a fellow Latino. Assuming that I was Jewish (though in fact not all Latinos are Roman Catholic, and all major religious denominations are represented among them), he once told me that I dressed very well, noting, "Jews dress nice. When Mexicans try to dress up in suits they end up looking like clowns."

When dealing with one of the few Latinos who feel as this man did about their native culture, attempts to show cultural sensitivity by acting respectfully formal or asking about his or her family, for example, are likely to offend. With such an individual, the most effective approach is to treat him as what he wishes to be: a member of the dominant Anglo culture; address him informally, introduce him by his occupation (for example, "This is my friend who is an architect."), and focus on his interests and accomplishments, rather than on his family.

Few Latinos reject their culture, however, and less acculturated Latinos generally respond gratefully to gestures of cultural accommodation. Those who are uncomfortable speaking English are almost always pleased when you make an effort, even an unsuccessful one, to speak their language. Latinos also usually feel that it is a compliment to them personally when respect and interest in their culture is shown.

Latinos who have been in the United States for many years have usually learned many of the nuances of Anglo culture, and thus achieved a degree of acculturation. Those who are more newly arrived generally must struggle not only with the difficulty of learning a new culture, but also with the feeling of being outsiders. Coming from a culture in which a sense of belonging is so central may make the acculturation process especially difficult for the Latino immigrant. Like previous immigrants to the United States, it is only the powerful promise of a better life that leads Latinos to leave their homes and learn to survive in a new culture.

Cross-Cultural Romances

MI:

When I moved to Guatemala in 1974, I found relations between men and women to be very different there than in the United States. Women in the U.S. were struggling with ambivalence about their roles, and increasingly concerned that acting "feminine" would be interpreted by men as indicating their acceptance of subservience. Guatemalan women appeared to feel no such ambivalence, and they doted on men. Most dressed with great style and flirted outrageously. Virtually all looked forward eagerly to being wives and mothers, even if they had career aspirations as well.

I was charmed by the femininity of Guatemalan women, and enthusiastically dated several. Then I met Colombina. We both worked for a World Health Organization research institute, but we didn't meet until the earthquake of 1976 occurred. One of the worst earthquakes of the twentieth century, it killed nearly 30,000 Guatemalans and destroyed whole villages. Colombina and I were assigned to the same rescue group sent to the Oriente, a desert area located in the eastern portion of the country, to assist people left homeless by the earthquake.

My attraction to Colombina was immediate. She is a beautiful woman who was extremely popular with her coworkers. Colombina had been both a star player on the national champion women's high-school basketball team, as well as a runner-up for Miss Guatemala, and I found the combination of her charming manner and enjoyment in being attractive, plus her independence and competitive spirit intoxicating.

After two years in Guatemala, I had learned a few things about romance, and when we set up a large tent for the rescue workers to sleep in on the first night of our mission, I moved my bedroll to the cot next to Colombina's. When it grew dark I took her hand, surrounded by our 30 coworkers. She later told me that she was shocked by my audacity, but she was also intrigued.

Colombina also told me that she was impressed by the fact that I left my family to travel all the way to Guatemala. The only one of her sisters to leave her small town in the Guatemalan highlands to work in the capitol, she had grown up expecting to eventually establish her home near her parents. However, she had also dreamed of seeing the world outside her country.

Colombina also said that my directness and informality made her feel able to be herself with me and to talk about anything without embarrassment, which gave our time together a sense of adventure and excitement for her. Her previous novio, like most Latino men, had always been very formal and proper around her, and expected her to be equally formal and proper.

By the time our group returned to the capitol a week later, we wanted to be novios. I was prepared to announce our intentions to our friends and families immediately, but Colombina was not. I did not yet understand that in her culture, romantic relationships were the direct concern of not only the couple in love, but also their extended families and close-knit communities, and that ending a romantic relationship and beginning another were actions that affected the lives of many people.

Fortunately, Colombina insisted on discretion. With kindness and tact, she ended her relationship in a manner that was least hurtful to her novio and his family, and began preparing her family members to accept this Nortéamericano into their very traditional Latino family. She was successful in her efforts, and we were married a year after we met, in one of the grandest social events in her town's memory.

When men and women meet and spend time together, they may be struck by Cupid's arrow, and fall in love. As the border between Latin America and the United States is increasingly crossed, bringing Anglos and Latinos together, cross-cultural romances and marriages happen.

Most people make the conventional choice of marrying their own kind. To do otherwise involves not only acting unconventionally, but also facing the unknown. When people do marry outside their own culture, they often believe that this will allow them to escape the restrictions of their culture. They have the fantasy that a cross-cultural romance will be "low maintenance." The reality is that cross-cultural romances are "high maintenance." They require hard work to overcome differences.

Latinas Are Fine

Anglo men are often attracted to Latinas, and this is not difficult to understand. Latinas typically feel very secure in their femininity and comfortable in expressing their interest in men. Most place a high priority on dressing attractively. Most also have excellent social skills and consider putting others at ease an important part of their femininity. Latinas typically possess other appealing qualities as well. Their strong family ties and religious upbringing give them a secure identity and a clear sense of right and wrong. Taught to work hard, most also know how to let loose and play as well.

Latinas are also often attracted to Anglo men. Many like Anglo men's freedom, informality, and openness. Many also appreciate their reliability; when a typical Anglo date tells a woman that he will pick her up at eight, he will arrive at eight. A Latino date may be much less concerned about punctuality in social situations; if he is occupied with another activity, he is unlikely to worry about when he arrives.

Mutual Irritation

Ironically, cross-cultural romances often fail because the same qualities that attracted the couple to one another in the first place eventually drive them crazy. For example, the Latina's strong sense of her own femininity, which many Anglo men find so attractive, may make her unwilling to assume the major responsibility for making a decision for her family. Even if she knows what she wants a decision to be, she expects her husband to take the responsibility for making it, because that is a man's job. Her Anglo husband may tire of shouldering this burden.

In addition, the Latina's responsibilities to her parents and relatives may create conflicts with her Anglo husband, because it makes her less available to him. Much more so than is the case for Anglo women, Latinas are expected to assist in any crises that occur in their immediate or extended families. They are also expected to share the burden of social functions given by family members. If her mother, sister, aunt, or niece is hosting a large party, a Latino woman is expected to assist, and her female relatives can be called on to do the same for her.

The Latina's charming social manner and her enjoyment in helping others is also likely to result in her devoting a great deal of time and energy to her friends and neighbors, reducing even more her time and energy available for her husband. Still other conflicts may arise because her sense of moral certainty may make her more insistent than her Anglo husband on conforming to the moral code with which she was raised. Even young Latinas who pride themselves on being liberal are often more unwilling than their Anglo husbands to entertain new beliefs and ideas that clash with those of their parents.

The Latina who marries an Anglo may also find that the qualities she found charming in him later become a source of irritation to her. His informality may come to be seen as crudeness and his openness as tactlessness. The freedom and individuality that allowed him to become independent of his family of origin may eventually be seen as selfishness. His openness to new ideas and willingness to modify moral standards may be seen as a lack of conviction and morality. Even his punctuality and reliability may later be seen by his Latina wife as a lack of spontaneity, or even as obsessiveness.

MI:

Colombina and I experienced some of these disillusionments. After a few years of marriage, I began to resent her insistence that I always take the responsibility for choosing the restaurant or the movie. Because she expected me to make a choice that would please her, I felt that I was being placed in a no-win situation; if I succeeded, that was assumed to be merely my responsibility. If I failed, then I was inconsiderate or insensitive to her wishes, and therefore failing in my responsibilities as a husband.

Colombina's certainty about what she believed also began to cause problems for me. Because her convictions were more firmly rooted than mine, she experienced our disagreements as a challenge to who she was, and they were therefore very upsetting to her. I found that if I argued effectively that she was wrong, I offended her sense of dignity. I soon learned that I could not win an argument with Colombina, because if I won, I lost.

Even her graciousness to everyone, which I greatly admired, began to cause difficulties in our relationship. She seemed unwilling to say no to people, and was always ready to help out. As a result, she was often occupied when our children and I would have liked her undivided attention.

Our difficulties were not one-sided. Though she had been attracted by my openness, she began to see that openness as a lack of tact. She felt that I was at times hurtful toward others, and disrespectful of her. As our children grew up, she was often upset by their lack of respeto *(respect), the primary obligation that every Latino child owes to his or her parents. She attributed our daughter's and son's lack of* respeto *to my influence, as well as that of Anglo culture. Like their Anglo classmates, our children were assertive in expressing disagreement with us, and sometimes they were simply rude. This usually upset Colombina much more than me, probably because I could remember acting the same way with my parents.*

Tall, Dark, and Handsome

Just as Anglo men are frequently attracted to Latino women, Latino men are often attracted to Anglo women. Many find Anglo women's independence and lack of concern about "*que pensará la gente?*" (what will people think?) exciting. They are also intrigued by the typical Anglo woman's more open interest in sex, since such interest must be carefully hidden by well-brought-up Latinas. "Shotgun marriages," demanded by a woman's family, all but disappeared in the United States a hundred years ago. However, they are common in Latin America, where a woman who is known to have had sex is considered ruined, even if she is not pregnant. She will not be considered an acceptable wife by most traditional Latino families, and her behavior is considered a disgrace to her family unless she marries her lover.

Anglo women are also frequently attracted to Latino men. Latino culture permits men to express their emotions and to act spontaneously more than Anglo culture does. The combination of expressiveness, spontaneity, and confidence in their masculinity typically found in Latino men is very attractive to many Anglo women. In addition to being more openly romantic than most Anglo men, most Latino men, having been raised by mothers who were both indulgent and demanding, are sensitive to the moods and desires of women. This too is very appealing to many Anglo women, who are also often attracted by the strong family ties of the Latino man, especially if their own families are not close.

SR:

Beth and I met at Penn State University. We took a class together and she conscientiously took detailed notes while I was socializing with classmates and taking hardly any notes at all. I admired how serious and well-organized she was. I was also intrigued by her confidence and independence. I wanted to meet her and was pleased when I found her in the company of a friend of mine in the library.

My Anglo friend failed to introduce us, then further frustrated me by declining to have coffee with me, even when I offered to buy him a piece of pie. He explained that he was on a diet. I told him that he wasn't fat or even chubby, then surprised an already amused Beth (who had intuited that my attention was focused on her, rather than my friend), by pinching her cheek and saying, "Now that's chubby!" Fortunately, as Beth later confided, she was delighted by my sometimes outrageous, outgoing way with people, which contrasted sharply with the withdrawal and obsessive focus on their studies of many of our fel-low students.

From that point, our courtship followed a Latino, rather than an Anglo, pattern. We didn't begin with awkward first dates, but got to know each other as members of an informal group of students who joined a popular professor for coffee after class. In Latino fashion, our relationship began in a group of friends, then progressed to becoming a couple, rather than beginning as a couple who later included their friends.

As I got to know Beth better, I learned that she belonged to a close and loving family. For example, unlike most out-of-state students, who would drive themselves to the university or come with friends, her father always drove her to campus at the beginning of each semester, and picked her up at the end of the semester.

Nevertheless, my Latino family was an even closer one, in which even difficult or obnoxious relatives were tolerated, and extended family visiting was constant and spontaneous. Beth was intrigued by my large, exuberant family, which immediately began treating her like one of them. When she met my father, he matter-of-factly asked her if she was going to marry me. When she said that she didn't know, he didn't give up, but asked if she liked me enough to marry me. She admitted that she did. When we traveled to Colombia after our wedding, my relatives teased her by asking why she wasn't a blonde, since I didn't have to go all the way to the United States to get a morenita *(a dark-complexioned woman).*

Our differences eventually caused problems in our relationship. I didn't always get home when Beth expected me, and I resented her efforts to control my time so closely. Beth felt that I gave too freely of my time and energies to people and organizations that requested them. "Shouldn't your family come first?" she often asked. I replied with equal conviction that you couldn't raise a family without a strong community, and I felt an obligation to contribute to our community.

Though she had been impressed by my family's net of interrelated-ness, Beth also began to tire of that net. Adolescent nephews who were exasperating their parents began to arrive from Colombia for extended stays. At first, each was charming and helpful around the house. How-ever, being adolescents, each eventually began exasperating us as they had their parents. Things reached a crisis point for Beth when sixteen of my relatives all arrived for Christmas one year, and it was impossible to walk through the house at night without stepping on a sleeping person. I understood her feelings, but as Beth rebelled, I nevertheless felt caught in the middle, and resented her unwillingness to accept my familial obligations as her own.

More Mutual Irritation

Just as occurs in couples made up of an Anglo man and a Latina, the same qualities that intrigue and attract Latino men and Anglo women to each other often cause problems in their relationships. Some Latino men come to resent the independence of their Anglo wives, who often refuse to accept the Latino arrangement in which the husband, as nominal head of the household, is the decision-maker. Under this arrangement, the husband does not make decisions unilaterally, but his wife's considerable influence on his decisions is expected to be communicated subtly, behind the scenes.

Latino men may also become uncomfortable with their Anglo wives' lesser concern about the good opinions of neighbors, friends, or even relatives. Well-brought-up Latino men and women are often concerned about appearances and the good opinions of others to a degree that may make them seem superficial or hypocritical to their Anglo spouses.

Latino men may even come to find their Anglo wives' open interest in sex, which seemed so exciting at first, disturbing or threatening to their masculinity. Within Latino culture, it is expected to be the man who initiates sex, and Latino men are accustomed to leading, rather than following, in the dance of intimacy.

The Anglo wife may become equally disillusioned with her Latino husband. Once charmed by his spontaneity, she may tire of it. She probably was thrilled when he bought her two dozen long-stemmed roses or impulsively whisked her away to San Francisco for a weekend during their courtship. However, once they are married, she may become very unhappy with his impulsive spending of money that is needed for other things.

She is also likely to resent his more relaxed approach to scheduling his time; he is likely to be less precise about when he will come home and less conscientious about coordinating his time with hers than the typical Anglo husband. She may become unhappy about his being so free in giving his time to others, at the cost of time with her. What she originally saw as an attractive social sensitivity in her Latino husband may come to be seen as a burdensome need to please others.

Her Latino husband's close ties to his family may also cause conflict in their marriage. As a well-brought-up Latino, he is expected to respond to the crises that occur in his extended family. His Anglo wife may resent the sacrifices she must make when her husband takes in family members or uses limited family resources to help out his relatives when they are in need.

Overcoming Cultural Differences

Given the potential for misunderstandings and conflict in Anglo-Latino relationships, it seems amazing that any survive. Some do not. Knowing from the beginning of their relationship about the ways their culture has shaped each's attitudes and behavior can help an Anglo-Latino couple to survive. That knowledge destroys the fantasy that there is a "right way" to think, or feel, or act; the "right way" depends on what culture you happened to be born into.

Not having that knowledge helped to destroy the marriage of an Albuquerque engineer and his Mexican-born wife. They had met in Mexico, experienced the strong mutual attraction that Anglos and Latinos often feel for each other, and married after a brief, whirlwind courtship. Mutual disillusionment set in almost immediately. He felt that she had married him as a meal ticket, because she quickly resigned from her job in order to start having children and care for her husband and home. She became angry and jealous when he spent long hours at work, and she assumed (incorrectly) that he was having affairs. Though he spoke decent college Spanish, neither really understood the other, and the couple lived together in increasing bitterness until obtaining a messy divorce a few years later.

Even if they are forewarned about their cultural differences, the Anglo-Latino couple must work hard to make their relationship successful. The power of our cultural conditioning is so strong that when our spouse behaves toward us in a way that is very different from how we were taught that people should behave, it is likely to cause us unintended hurt or insult.

This makes it even more imperative than for other couples that Anglo-Latino couples learn to talk and listen to each other. They need to learn to avoid personal attacks ("You're selfish"), universal statements ("You always do that to me"), and moral judgment statements ("People shouldn't act like that"). They need instead to learn to focus on the behavior that upset them and to explain how that behavior made them feel ("When you came home late, it made me feel neglected and sad").

Even more so than other couples, Anglo-Latino couples must also learn to compromise. Some issues, such as the importance of fidelity or the religious instruction of children, may be non-negotiable, and need to be discussed openly before permanent commitments are made. But most conflicts because of cultural differences can be avoided or minimized through discussion, a sense of humor, and eventual compromise. Every happy marriage involves each spouse accepting that there are some things about their partner that they cannot change, and some things about themselves that they must.

MI:

Colombina and I have finally been able to reach a middle ground on the issue of responsibility for day-to-day decision making. Oddly enough, larger decisions, such as what house or car to buy, have always been easier for us, because Colombina has been more willing to express her views about these. I am still expected to choose the restaurant or movie. However, Colombina no longer blames me if she is disappointed in my choices, because she has learned that I can't always anticipate what she will like. She is also less often disappointed in my choices, because I've learned to better anticipate what she will like.

Disagreements are still difficult for us, though considerably less so than when we were first married. After many years together, we've become more alike. We now disagree less often. When we do, now Colombina sometimes discusses our disagreements with me instead of pouting, and I sometimes hold my tongue instead of confronting her. I appreciate her telling me what she thinks as much as she appreciates me not doing so.

SR:

Beth and I have also found ways to compromise about our differences. I have learned to accept that being more available and accountable to her is important to Beth. Beth has come to accept that my being very involved in our community is important to me. We don't always agree on the extent of that involvement, but we talk about it and usually manage to find a middle ground.

We have also compromised on the issue of family obligations. As they aged, Beth's parents began spending summers in our city, and then moved their home here, as my widowed mother had already done. Beth has come to embrace the Latino concept of the "expanding table," grateful for the opportunity to make our parents a part of our daily lives.

At the same time, I have learned to set some limits on our involvement with my extended family. Though earlier in our marriage we helped to raise three of my Colombian nephews when their parents needed help, we have recently declined the opportunity to take in other adolescent relatives. As Beth has turned more outward toward our extended families, I have learned to focus more of my attention on our immediate family.

Anglo-Latino relationships are more difficult than relationships between two Anglos or two Latinos. For couples who are able to grow and change, they are also worth the extra effort. It is not by chance that Anglos and Latinos are often so attracted to each other; they seem to somehow know that each completes the other. Where many Anglos have difficulty with commitment, connection, and tact, most Latinos are sure of what they believe, intensely loyal, and tactful. Where many Latinos have difficulty with open-mindedness, independence, and confrontation, most Anglos are open-minded, independent, and willing to disagree. In a successful Anglo-Latino relationship, each partner becomes both a teacher and a student. By absorbing each other's strengths, each is given the freedom to transcend the limitations of their own culture.

Conclusion

Latino migration is resulting in increasing contact between Latinos and mainstream Americans in workplaces, schools, businesses, and neighborhoods across the United States. Our purpose in writing the *Invisible Border* has been to make these interactions more positive ones, by helping to make Latino culture more understandable to Anglos, and Anglo culture less confusing to Latinos. Mutual understanding provides no guarantee of successful relationships between Anglos and Latinos, but it can reduce misunderstandings based on ignorance, and the mistrust and suspicion that result from such misunderstandings.

As developmental psychologists, we have focused on the ways that families, the basic units of each culture, prepare their children to be successful in their society, encouraging those qualities and behaviors which their culture values, and discouraging those that their culture disdains. We have tried to show that cultural differences do not result from one group being better or worse than another, but are the logical outcome of the efforts of good families to prepare their children to flourish as adults.

Our own lives have been enriched by having lived in two cultures, and we believe that our country has also benefitted from its multicultural heritage. The history of the United States makes a strong argument that the arrival of successive groups of immigrants from many cultures energizes and enriches a nation.

In addition to these benefits, Latino immigration to the United States may bring with it an unexpected bonus. A surprising complementarily results from the fact that Anglo culture strongly emphasizes individuality and individual achievement, while Latino culture places an equally strong emphasis on relationships and cooperation. Each group can learn much from the other, and Anglo-Latino relationships have the potential to be uniquely successful and productive.

Bibliography

Anaya, Rudolfo. 1999. *Bless Me Ultima*. Boston, MA: Warner Books.

Baldwin, James. 1952. *Go Tell it on the Mountain*. New York, NY: Dell.

Bates, Stephen. 2004. "Vatican Birth Control Policy Spurned." *The Guardian*, 30 June.

Beltleheim, Bruno. 1980. *Surviving and Other Essays*. New York, NY: Vintage Books.

Bowler, Sharon, Stephen Nicholson, and Gary Segura. 2006. "Earthquakes and Aftershocks: Tracking Partisan Identification amid California's Changing Political Environment." *American Journal of Political Science* 50(1):146-59.

Calvin, John. 1989. *Institutes of the Christian Religion*. Grand Rapids, MI: William B. Eerdmans.

Constable, Pamela. 2007. "Latinos Unite to Turn Fear into Activism". *The Washington Post*, 28 July.

Cervantes, Miguel de. 2003. *Don Quixote*. Translated by Edith Grossman. *New York, NY: Harper Collins*.

Chambers, Marcia. 1998. "Golf: Nike Has its Money on Both Sides of Disability Dispute." *The New York Times*, 2 February.

Chong, Nilda, and Francia Baez. 2005. *Latino Culture: A Dynamic Force in the Changing American Workplace*. Yarmouth, ME: Intercultural Press.

Clinton, Hillary Rodham. 1996. *It Takes a Village*. New York, NY: Touchstone.

Condon, Peter. 2007. "Knownothingism." In *The Catholic Encyclopedia*, Volume VIII. New York, NY: Robert Appleton Company.

Del Aguila, Juan M. 1999. "Reflections on a Non-Transition in Cuba: Comments on Elites". *Papers and Proceedings of the Ninth Annual Conference on Cuba in Transition*, Volume 9:192-200.

Dickler, Jessica. 2007. "Best Paid Executives: The Gender Gap Exaggerated." *CNN/money.com*, 3 October.

Dowd, Maureen. 1997. "Liberties; Promises, Promises, Promises." *The New York Times*, 4 October.

Einstein, Albert. 1952. "Letter to Jacques Hadamard" In *The Creative Process*, Edited by Brewster Ghiselin. New York, NY: Mentor 43-44.

Engler, Mark. 2007. "America's Own Worst Enemy". *The New York Times*, 6 March.

Federation for American Immigration Reform. 2004. "U.S. Immigration History." www.fairus.org.

Garcia Marquez, Gabriel. 1970. *One Hundred Years of Solitude*. New York, NY: Harper and Row.

Garcia, F. Chris and Gabriel R. Sanchez. *Hispanics and the U.S. Political System: Moving into the Mainstream*. Upper Saddle River, NJ: Pearson Prentice Hall.

García, John A. 2003. *Latino Politics in America: Community, Culture, and Interests*. Lanham, MD: Rowman and Littlefield.

Hernández, Mario. 2005. "Deberán Pagar Aguinaldos antes del 20 de Diciembre." *La Crónica de Hoy*, 2 December.

Hersh, Seymour. 1998. *The Dark Side of Camelot*. Boston, MA: Little, Brown and Company.

Highton, Benjamin, and Arthur L. Burris. 2002. "New Perspectives on Latino Voter Turnout in the United States." *American Politics Research* 30(3): 285-306.

Hispanic PR Wire. 2007. "Latino Issues Forum Announces New Leadership." 10 September.

Hummel, Ruth. 1994. *Where do Babies Come From?* St. Louis, MO: Concordia Publishing House.

King, Carole. 1971. "So Far Away." On *Tapestry*. Ode/Epic/Legacy.

Klapper, Bradley S. 2007. "Americans Produce, Work More." *Albuquerque Journal*, 3 September.

Lacey, Marc. 2006. "A Rare Silence Reverberates in Castro's Long Goodbye." *The New York Times*, 2 December.

Larmer, Brook, and Rod Nordland. 1998. "Preaching to the Masses." *Newsweek*. 131.n.5 (2 February 1998):54(4).

Lester, David. 2000. "The Epidemiology of Suicide. In *"Suicide Prevention: Resources for the Millenium,"* edited by David Lester. Philadelphia, PA: Brunner Routledge, pp. 3-16.

Lindman, Maj. 1995. *Snipp, Snapp, and Snurr and the Buttered Bread.* Morton Grove, IL: Albert Whitman & Company.

Mack, F.R. Poncefonte and Thomas E. Jackson. 1993. *Teacher Education as a Career Choice of Hispanic High School Students.* Grand Rapids, MI: Grand Rapids Public Schools.

McGirk, Jon. January. 2002. "Millions Greet Pope in Mexico City." *The Sunday Independent,* 1 August.

Ngowi, Rodrique. 2007. "Parents Begin Potty Training at Birth." *Farmington Daily Times,* 28 August.

North, Don. 2002. "The Colombian Drug Quagmire," *Foreign Service Journal.* January 2002.

Piper, Watty. 1995. *The Little Engine That Could.* New York, NY: Philomel Books.

Potter, George Ann and Linda Farthing. 2000. "Bolivia: Eradication and Backlash." *Foreign Policy in Focus* 5, no. 38.

President's Advisory Commission on Educational Excellence for Hispanic Americans. 1999. *One Nation on the Fault Line.* Washington, D.C.: U.S. Government Printing Office.

Schacter, Jason P. 2004. *Geographical Mobility: 2002 to 2004 Population Characteristic,* pp. 20-549, March 2004, disc.wisc.edu/reports/CDERE/cderr25.ltm; Why People Move: Exploring the March 2000 Current Population Survey-U.S. Census Bureau.

Schlessinger, Laura C. 1996. *How Could You Do That?!* New York, NY: Harper Collins.

Schmidt, Peter. 2003. "Academe's Hispanic Future." *Chronicle Special Report* 50(14):A8.

Smith, Tony. 1991. "The Alliance for Progress: The 1960's." In *Exporting Democracy: The United States and Latin America,* edited by Abraham F. Lowenthal. Baltimore, MD: The Johns Hopkins University Press. pp. 71-89.

Tichenor, Daniel J. 2007. Testimony before U.S. House of Representatives Committee on the Judiciary, Subcommittee on Immigration, Refugees, Border Security, and International Law, March 30, 2007. http://judiciary.house.gov/media/pdfs/tichenor 07 03 30.

Twain, Mark. 2005. *Huckleberry Finn.* Cheswald, DE: Prestwick House.

U.S. Census Bureau. 2007. "Population of the United States by Race and Hispanic/Latino Origin, Census 2000 and July 1, 2005." From: Infoplease. www.infoplease.com/ipa/A0762156 (accessed 24 January 2008).

Velez, Wanda A. 1990. "South American Immigration: Argentina." In *The Autobiographical Mode in Latin American Literature I.* Yale-New Haven Teachers Institute.

Zeidel, Robert F. 2004. *Immigrants, Progressives, and Exclusion Polititics: The Dillingham Commission, 1900-1927.* DeKalb, IL: Northern Illinois University Press.

Zuckebrod, Nancy. 2007. "Illegal Students Await Immigration Plan." USA Today, 3 June.

Index